Science and the Theory of Value

STUDIES IN PHILOSOPHY

CONSULTING EDITOR: *V. C. Chappell*

THE UNIVERSITY OF CHICAGO

Science and the Theory of Value

PETER CAWS

HUNTER COLLEGE OF THE
CITY UNIVERSITY OF NEW YORK

RANDOM HOUSE NEW YORK

FIRST PRINTING

Published in New York by Random House, Inc. and simultaneously in Toronto, Canada, by Random House of Canada Limited.
Library of Congress Catalog Card Number: 67–18128
Manufactured in the United States of America by
THE COLONIAL PRESS, INC., CLINTON, MASS.

TYPOGRAPHY BY LEON BOLOGNESE

PREFACE

This book has been written in the conviction that a great deal of what has been learned since the scientific revolution of the sixteenth and seventeenth centuries is regularly left out of account in dealing with problems of value. I have in mind less the facts discovered by science (important as they are) than the principles of empirical knowledge which the discovery of those facts has brought to light. The significant thing about science is that it is knowledge attained, organized, and established in a certain way. It has seemed worth while to inquire whether knowledge about value might not be attained, organized, and established in an analogous way and to ask further, if so, what such knowledge might consist of.

The answer to these questions, as it emerges in what follows, is that the structure of scientific knowledge can, *mutatis mutandis*, be transferred to our knowledge of values, although the necessary changes lead to a crucial difference between the two kinds of knowledge. Value can be furnished with an empirical warrant while still retaining its distinctive character as value. The theory of value does not become a science, but it appropriates some of the methods of science and no longer needs to depend on theological or political or romantic presuppositions. And in this way it achieves a basis for universality and a practical relevance which are urgently needed.

The material presented here has formed the substance of courses given at the University of Kansas in the fall of 1963 and at the New School for Social Research in the spring of 1965, and I am indebted to my students for many comments and suggestions. The manuscript has been read by a number of friends and colleagues, among whom my special thanks are due to Vere Chappell, Abraham Edel, Stuart Hampshire, Charles Landesman, Jr., Ernest Nagel, and John Pfeiffer for criticism and encouragement in various forms. In particular I owe to Jim Landesman the argument which appears on page 84, although I am afraid it deserves better elaboration than I have given it there.

I am grateful to President John Meng of Hunter College and to the Abbey and Nora Scholarship Fund for a grant for secretarial expenses. The burden of the preparation of the manuscript has been shared at various times by Rita Breitbart, Carol Ann Liebich, Mrs. Laura Moore, and Mrs. Joan Wicks, and I wish to thank them also. Finally, by the continuity of her interest, as well as by frequent help on individual points, my wife has made a greater contribution than anyone.

PETER CAWS

New York, *November 1966*

CONTENTS

Science and the Theory of Value

I

The Utility of Moral Argument

A NEGLECTED FUNCTION OF MORAL PHILOSOPHY. The central purpose of this book is to redefine the scope and foundation of moral judgment. Its method borrows what can be borrowed from science, and one of its ancillary purposes is, therefore, to determine what the limits of such borrowing are and to distinguish between the proper objects of scientific theory and of the theory of value. The great majority of recent writers on ethics have proceeded inductively, attempting to extract from common beliefs or common uses of language the general principles of morality or the paradigmatic meanings of terms like "good" and "right." These attempts have usually led to the identification of the highest object of moral endeavor with a philosophical *summum bonum:* pleasure, the intellectual love of God, the greatest happiness of the greatest number, progress, the classless society, the performance of one's duty, self-realization, or engagement in an authentic project. The overwhelming impression left by a survey of this literature is that nobody is entirely confident about the range of phenomena to be dealt with by moral philosophy, although everybody is prepared to recognize some set of problems, more or less pressing in his own times or circumstances, as distinctively moral. And while analyses of such familiar problems of moral behavior generally come out right, in that they accord with common sense, for the most part it is clearly the common sense which dictates the analysis and not, as might have been hoped, the analysis which justifies the common sense.

It may be argued, of course, that it is not the business of the moral philosopher to justify anything, but that his analysis is a second-order activity with no commitment to one moral conclusion rather than another. Some such caveat is to be found in many works on ethics. But in ethics, of all the branches of philosophy, such detachment is virtually impossible. Ethics deals with the nature and justification of moral argument, and what makes an argument moral is never merely its form but always also the use to which it is to be put and the practical consequences of that use. Moral arguments must be of use in the solution of moral problems, and the philosopher's decision as to what counts as a moral problem and what does not already commits him, more or less explicitly, to some ethical position or other. Philosophers have as a rule tended to disclaim any such commitment, taking up rather the position of disengaged critics, out of a natural reluctance to assume an apparent moral superiority over other men, which might involve hypocrisy if they failed to live exemplary lives. "Be not too hasty to trust, or to admire, the teachers of morality," says Dr. Johnson; "they discourse like angels, but they live like men." [1] This reluctance, however, rests on a confusion: the commitment to an ethical position is not a moral commitment but an intellectual one, and the philosopher's life belongs to a different logical category from his teachings. A thoroughly immoral man might propound a correct moral theory, and it would be correct nonetheless. The theory would condemn him, as it would condemn any other man who acted similarly, but the fact that it was *his* theory would not make the condemnation any worse. His behavior might, it is true, have something to do with the attitude that other people took to the theory, but if they rejected it for the wrong reasons that would be their affair.

The moral philosopher need not hesitate, therefore, to make recommendations about, as well as impartial assessments of, the various arguments with which he deals. But if moral arguments are to be useful in the solution of moral problems, they must first of all be intelligible to people who confront moral problems. Since everybody confronts moral problems, this makes a demand on ethics more stringent than any demand made, for example, on metaphysics or logic or the philosophy of science. It might be pointed out that everybody confronts scientific problems too, but this overlooks an important point. Science is a refinement of ordinary experience, and the common-sense solutions which ordinary men find to the commonplace problems which arise in their dealings with the physical world are not yet scientific. But morality is *part* of ordinary experience, and many of the commonplace problems of ordinary men, which arise in their deal-

[1] Samuel Johnson, *The History of Rasselas, Prince of Abyssinia* (New York: Home Book Co., n.d.), p. 90.

ings with other people, are full-blown moral phenomena which require no refinement in order to become the subject of ethical discussion. This does not mean that there is no room in ethics for technicalities and refinements, but it does mean that these must always be secondary to the main task, which is the construction and criticism of arguments relevant to the concerns of ordinary men and robust enough to withstand the uses to which ordinary men will put them. There is, it is true, nothing to prevent a philosopher from spending his life in secondary activity; in fact that can be, as Broad remarks, "quite good fun for those people who like that sort of thing."[2] And too evangelical a tone is not considered good form among philosophers. But perhaps, in spite of professional qualms, the time has come for philosophy to take upon itself the authority in moral matters to which religion and nationalism have proved unequal; and if so it must be ready to provide arguments capable of carrying everyday burdens, as well as arguments suitable to the more recondite interests of professors.

CRITERIA FOR A PRACTICALLY USEFUL MORAL THEORY. That, however, is not nearly as easy as it looks. The specifications of arguments which meet the conditions are formidable. Their premises must be generally accessible and convincing; their terms must be unambiguous and generally intelligible; their steps must be generally plausible, and such that they can be easily followed; their applicability to cases must be plain; but they must be analytically rigorous. It is quite true that large numbers of arguments apparently satisfying these criteria have been in practical use for a long time, but their success has been due to an overloading

[2] C. D. Broad, *Five Types of Ethical Theory* (London: Routledge and Kegan Paul, 1930), p. 285.

of the premises—with religious or patriotic, but always emotive, material—to such an extent that the argument itself becomes a mere appendage. The fear of God or the love of country, together with some set of commandments or exhortations, can be relied on to solve all moral problems whatever, once the premises are accepted. There may of course be disagreements about the interpretation of the premises, but these have usually been treated as theological or political, rather than philosophical, matters. And yet this problem of the premises is one of the most crucial in ethics. It has often been supposed that the task of the moral philosopher would be done if the meanings of the terms used in moral argument could be clarified and the rigor of such argument guaranteed. But the analysis of "*x* is good," for example, may show that the acceptance of such a judgment involves some belief—about the nature of man, perhaps, or the grounds of obligation—which stands as an implicit premise of every argument involving the term "good"; if this belief were not held, the meaning of the term would be altogether changed. If there were valid reasons for supposing the belief to be groundless or compelling, the analysis would hardly count as complete if they were not specified.

The ultimate premises of moral argument are moral principles, and it is here that the greatest confusion, both popular and professional, is to be found. On the popular level there is general dismay at the failure of the old principles and the lack of satisfactory replacements for them, so that it comes to be believed either that there are no principles or—what amounts to the same thing—that principles must once again be taken on blind faith. On the professional level there is a curious reluctance either to be forthright in discarding the old principles or to be imaginative in proposing new ones. Scholarly disengagement is once more a convenient excuse: descriptive ethics exhibits the principles that men have in fact adhered to at various times and in various places, but it need not pass judgment on them; the analysis of ethical language uncovers implicit presuppositions, but is more concerned about their logical relations to the rest of the system than about their truth. The solution to these difficulties does not lie in a further examination of the same data, whether behavioral or linguistic. What is required is a theoretical model for ethics, whose adequacy to the data is to be judged only after it has been worked out to a sufficient degree of complexity.

HYPOTHETICAL PRINCIPLES. The principles on which such a model rests will be hypothetical, but the hypotheses can be quite simple ones. For the purposes of its development the assertion of the hypotheses cannot help but appear dogmatic, but the dogmatism is relative: the principles are *a priori* with respect to the system, but the system itself is *a posteriori* with respect to empirical evidence. A distinction is to be drawn, however, between *a priori* principles (such as the principle of contradiction) necessary for the development of any system whatever, which are incorrigible in the light of empirical evidence because they are empirically empty, and functionally *a priori* principles necessary for the development of some particular system, which are corrigible in the light of empirical evidence, such evidence arising out of the adequacy or inadequacy to experience of the system as a whole.

Among functionally *a priori* principles a further distinction is to be drawn between two types which may be called respectively *elementary* and *transcendent*. Elementary principles have empirical content, in that they purport to refer to actual events, but they apply to such events distributively—that is, one at a time; the system is built up by considering what follows if events, taking place according to the principles, occur serially or simultaneously, with greater degrees of complexity, and so on. The principles of science—for example, of quantum mechanics or of genetics—are of this type, and the inclusion of such principles is a condition of the empirical relevance of any system. Transcendent principles, on the other hand, while they also purport to refer to actual events, apply somehow (and one of their characteristics is that the manner of this application is generally obscure) to the totality of events, often overlooking distinctions between *kinds* of event; and the system, instead of resting upon them, is constrained by them. In a system built up on the basis of elementary principles, a statement is admitted as true if it can be shown to follow from the principles; in a system developed in the light of transcendent principles, a statement is rejected as false if it cannot be reconciled with the principles, even though there may be no obvious connection between them and it. Most principles of metaphysics and religion—for example, the existence and goodness of God, the infallibility of the scriptures, or the purpose of history—are of this second type.

The logical form of transcendent principles is often existential, as these examples show; the logical form of elementary principles is always universal. Some confusion has arisen, however, because there are important elementary principles whose customary expression is apparently existential—for example, the assertions that there is an absolute zero of temperature or an absolute limit of velocity. But the velocity of light and the zero point of the Kelvin scale do not exist as God is alleged to exist; they limit actual processes distributively and can be formulated so as to avoid all reference to existence:

$$(x)\ (v)\ (x \text{ moves with velocity } v \supset v \leq c)$$
$$(x)\ (T)\ (\text{the temperature of } x \text{ is } T \supset T > 0°\text{K});$$

or in plain English: for every x and every v, if x moves with a velocity v then this velocity is less than or equal to that of light; and for every x and every T, if the temperature of x is T then this temperature is greater than zero Kelvin. In other words, nothing can move faster or be colder than these limits allow. When put in this way such principles cannot be confused with transcendent ones.

This distinction need not be pursued further; it was introduced only in order to clarify the nature of the system to be developed in the following chapters. Many ethical theories have added to their inductive generalizations an appeal to some transcendent principles, and the resulting uncertainty about the warrant for ethical recommendations, together with a tendency on the part of moralists to shift ground from one justification to the other in the course of argument, has seriously weakened the force and intellectual interest of the theories in question, and indirectly of ethics in general. The principles appealed to have not always been explicit; very often, in fact, the best critical intentions are not enough to prevent a covert appeal to principles whose personal or cultural roots are too deep to make their overt recognition possible, and it must in honesty be admitted that this remark may very well apply to the argument of this book. Usually, however, the function of transcendent principles has been more or less consciously—although with no sense of philosophical impropriety—to universalize conclusions based on merely local evidence; they have been extremely useful in stabilizing the local situations from which the evidence was drawn, but they have generally been disastrous when exported by well-meaning missionaries, and even their local use has frequently been repressive. Moreover, while I have included transcendent principles among functionally *a priori* principles capable of indirect empirical test, it must be admitted that they have customarily been employed in such a way as to exclude the possibility of empirical refutation. For example, the principle that God is good and desires the happiness of his creatures would appear to be inconsistent with the prevalence of misery in the world, but this argument may be effectively disposed of by reference to God's ineffable purpose.

THE REJECTION OF TRANSCENDENCE. For these and other reasons, transcendent principles are thoroughly unsatisfactory in the construction of a theory of morals. One man's orthodoxy is another man's heresy, and if conflicts are to be resolved, the reaffirmation of such principles is not the way to go about it. The motivation for a great deal of work in ethics is to be found in personal, institutional, or national situations of conflict, and that is why so many ethical theories are rationalizations of some status quo, ennobled by an appeal to the appropriate transcendent principle: democracy, the church, tradition, the revolution. But none of these will do for resolving the conflicts which now confront mankind, because each is the apotheosis of a localized belief and none carries universal conviction. We must have either universally shared transcendent principles or none at all. In the present circumstances the latter is the only available option. Accordingly we are left with elementary principles alone for the construction of our theory: the foundation of this theory must lie in what is immediately accessible to every individual, no matter what his situation in the world, and assumptions which transcend this are to be resolutely excluded.

This recommendation appears to conflict with the declared intention of proceeding hypothetically. There are two things to be said here: first, that antecedently plausible principles may be put forward hypothetically—in the sense that the theory stands ready to discard them, even though it does not expect to be called upon to do so—and second, that hypothetical principles stand a better chance of leading to fruitful systems if they are antecedently plausible. The example of science is again useful. Although some fairly recent scientific hypotheses—of quantum mechanics and of relativity, for example—seem quite implausible to simple people, so that science has often been represented to them as an affair of marvels and mysteries, the elementary principles through which the student is introduced to science are perfectly familiar and convincing in the light of ordinary experience. The components of the universe referred to by the principles may be smaller or larger than everyday objects and their properties may be unusual, but they are objects or regions in space and time and their properties are of a sort that can be exhibited in simple phenomena. Anybody who has ever held a couple of magnets in his hands should be ready for anything modern physics has to offer. The strength of science lies to a great degree in this accessibility of its basic hypotheses, from which by a series of stepwise moves the student may be led to the most remote or surprising of its truths.

This condition is of comparatively recent origin. Science got nowhere in its animistic and theological stages, not only because it lacked conceptual precision but also because the elements of experience on which it rested were just those that were most mysterious and implausible. This was especially true of chemistry and medicine, although even fairly advanced sciences like physics appealed to tendencies and powers verging on the occult. The principles invoked to account for these experiences were even more bizarre than the experiences themselves, so that credulity became a virtue without which orthodoxy was impossible. Something like this is still true in moral theory at the popular level; it is, for example, widely held that morality is impossible without religion. (This doctrine has, I believe, had an effect exactly opposite to what was intended and has weakened morality rather than strengthened it; for religion is now far less plausible to educated men than morality is in its own right, so that if morality is made to depend on it, rather than standing alone, the tendency is to discount the morality along with the religion and to assume that right behavior is no more important than ritual behavior.) It is also frequently assumed, even by professional philosophers, that the solution of moral problems requires an understanding of the nature of man, whatever that may mean. Of course if one starts out by posing an insoluble and possibly meaningless problem and refuses to proceed until it is solved, it is hardly surprising if the argument does not get very far. If science had insisted on understanding the nature of matter, for example, or of space, or of time, before tackling its other problems, we would still believe that the earth was at rest in the center of the universe. The nature of man may be the last thing we understand, and the most useful recent philosophical contribution to the debate about it has been the existentialists' assertion that there is no such thing, which while it is certainly too hasty has the virtue of cutting through a great deal of pious nonsense.

It must not be assumed, from the polemical tone of these remarks, that the position advocated here is necessarily anti-religious or anti-humanistic. Religion, and the softer brands of humanism, no doubt have their place; it is just that their place is not in the discussion of moral theory, since, in order to achieve universality, special assumptions must be excluded *even if they are right.* It is not enough to start from what is true—the starting point must be something that is *generally agreed* to be true, at least tentatively and for the purposes of argument. Clearly the widest agreement will be commanded by the smallest set of principles, so that the rule is to reduce the number to a minimum.

DOUBTS ABOUT HUMAN RATIONALITY. There is, however, one condition for the utility of moral argument that is independent of and indeed prior to any assumptions whatever in this sense, namely that argument should be an acceptable mode of procedure. If philosophy is motivated by any conviction—rather than by a kind of intellectual dilettantism—it is by the conviction that men ought to have reasons for acting as they act and for believing what they believe and that these reasons ought to be the best they can find. But if people are not persuaded by reasons, there is not much point in arguing with them. It is certainly not the case that all human beings are amenable to rational argument, and under special circumstances (in times of emergency, for example) reasoning has always had to be supplemented by coercion. History shows that this has happened far too often, but not that it was never necessary. Without going into the question of political freedom, which comes later in the book, it is clear that, if men are to be induced to behave in one way rather than another—morally rather than immorally—the chief alternative to coercion is rational persuasion. (Non-rational persuasion, such as propaganda or high-pressure advertising, counts as a form of coercion.) Moral argument is one important form of rational persuasion, and its utility will be seriously curtailed if rationality is not widespread.

It will not do, in search of reassurance on this point, to resort to the Aristotelian definition of man as the "rational animal." Rationality in the sense of being *able* to reason is in any case not enough; there must be a disposition to *use* the ability, a habitual recourse to it in situations which call for decision. The touching confidence with which philosophers always used to assume that this was in fact the case, at least whenever it really mattered, has been badly shaken by recent events, which constitute in the eyes of many people a crisis not only of value but of rationality itself. If things are really as bad as they are sometimes made to appear, philosophy cannot possibly be of any help, and it cannot help in any case if it is not known what the problems are which need to be solved. For both these reasons it will be as well, before going any further, to make a brief assessment of the contemporary situation.

II

The Contemporary Crisis of Value

STRAINS IN THE SYSTEM OF VALUES. Every age is considered by its contemporaries, or at least by some of them, to be an age of crisis, if only because the stable world in which fortunate children grow up turns out on mature inspection to be full of changes. It is hard to say how much of the current anxiety is to be attributed to this perennial discomfort, but even when the most generous allowance has been made for it the present age still seems to be suffering from a more acute crisis than previous ones. In fact it is in chronic crisis, which is not the contradiction in terms it appears to be. "Crisis" is a transliteration of the Greek for "decision," and crises go on until decisions are arrived at which change the situation. Our chronic condition is one of indecision; many questions—about man, nature, society, and God—which were once thought to have been finally decided have been reopened, and the bases for decisions about totally new problems, such as nuclear war and overpopulation, have hardly yet been established. We have learned to live with crisis, because fundamental decisions can nearly always be put off; but the longer they are put off, the more unpleasant the available alternatives may become. The trouble is that we wish to be sure that our decisions are right, and this requires a degree of certainty about the aims and the consequences of action to which we have not attained. The old certainty has gone; its demise was a long drawn out process which came to a foreseeable climax in the middle of this century. What was not foreseen was the eruption, at the same historical juncture, of grave new uncertainties. In the circumstances it is hardly surprising that the structure of values should be showing signs of strain, since value is an indispensable ingredient of decision, and any uncertainty about it spoils the whole decision-making process.

THE EFFECT OF THE POPULARIZATION OF SCIENCE. Once again this state of affairs manifests itself differently at the level of popular understanding and at the level of professional analysis. In the previous chapter it was said that these levels ought to be intimately connected where ethical questions are concerned, but that such a connection is not necessary in the case of scientific questions. Paradoxically, however, the connection has been established far more successfully in science than in ethics, and this fact itself contributes to the crisis. For popular understanding of science—which is often accurate enough—has rendered far more difficult than formerly the acceptance of the principles on which values depended for so long, and technology, the form in which science presents itself most obtrusively to the public, has transformed the environment to which those values were appropriate. The coincidence referred to above was not perhaps quite so fortuitous after all. And yet the attitude of science has been consistently benign; it did not set out to destroy faith, but rather to improve the condition of man. From the point of view of material well-being its success has been virtually complete; but the claims of the optimists of the turn of the century, who saw in science the final answer to all human problems, no longer seem even remotely valid.

In fact, while it is of course easy to exaggerate the seriousness of a critical situation, an impartial observer from another planet, reading only best-selling novels and the periodical press, would be likely to come to an extremely pessimistic conclusion about the human condition, the continued advance of science notwithstanding. The characteristic symptoms of the malaise of the age, he might conclude, are fear, anguish, loss of identity, alienation, and boredom. Fear and boredom are directly attributable to technological change, loss of identity to scientific developments; anguish and alienation are produced indirectly, as quasi-philosophical responses to scientific and technological stimuli. The scientific problem is the oldest, and it is a problem of contrasts, arising uniquely in a Western civilization brought up on Christianity. Man used to consider himself the child of God, specially created as the apotheosis of the natural order, compound of body and spirit, to whom the earth had been given as a central habitation and the heavens as a covering. He was shown, by Copernicus and later astronomers, that in fact he clings to a speck of matter, suspended in an infinite abyss, which is not particularly near the center of anything and provides only accidentally and temporarily an environment friendly to life; by Darwin that there is nothing special about his origins, but that he himself is an accidental, and again probably temporary, terminus of a random and unintelligent process; and by Freud and the anthropologists that his personal and social behavior is very largely determined by internal and external conditions whose origins he cannot remember and which he cannot control. Pascal was frightened by the infinite spaces; less humble representatives of the established order met the doctrines of evolution and psychoanalysis rather with indignation, but it was clear that they were frightened too.

THE EFFECT OF TECHNOLOGY. Of course there was no need to be frightened, at least not yet, for there is nothing inherently pessimistic about the view of man presented by modern science, and to argue from the new view of his circumstances and origins to a lessening of his stature is to succumb to the genetic fallacy. Intellectually, science put man at an unprecedented advantage with respect to nature, and at first it promised to do so practically as well. It is only quite recently that the possibility has had to be taken seriously that the insertion of scientific determinations into a complex network of human and natural causes and effects may have started chains of events that cannot be controlled. The two most familiar cases of this danger are, of course, the existence of nuclear weapons and the difficulty of preventing their use by irresponsible governments, and the lowering of the death rate by successful attacks on disease without a corresponding lowering of the birth rate. The race may eventually destroy itself by one method or the other if controls are not devised. But these dangers, serious as they are, are for the immediate future less pressing and less difficult to avert than a series of others which have arisen as indirect consequences of the application of science and technology to human affairs.

The rise of technology has had two effects on individuals, one having to do with their control of their world and one with their enjoyment of it, in regard to both of which the question of value arises in a fundamental way. First of all technology has transformed the production of material goods. In pre-industrial society the individual was not very far removed from the source of his material supplies, and if he himself did not control that source at least somebody obviously like him did—somebody with greater powers and privileges, perhaps, but somebody who could be met, and on occasion even conquered, at the level of man to man. Industrialization changed the situation irreversibly; social and political structures became for the first time genuinely inhuman, and human beings became alienated from them. The term "alienation" has in recent years become familiar in sophisticated conversation, and it is often assumed to be a special mark of the age, but the philosophical history of the term justifies this view only partially. Alienation, according to Hegel, is a necessary condition of consciousness; the object of consciousness must be different from, and over against, the conscious subject, and the emergence of consciousness and its ultimate reconciliation with its object is therefore a dialectical process of self-alienation. Every individual, in whatever age, goes through the process, so there is nothing remarkable in the fact that contemporary man does so. The alienation of the individual takes place within a larger framework which is not thereby deprived of its unity. But Marx raised the possibility that the object, which originally depended on consciousness for its constitution as an object, may become autonomous and turn on its creator. Social and political institutions, for example—certainly human constructions—may enter on careers that human intervention, at least at the individual level, is powerless to stop or even to influence. The institutions of which this state of affairs is most characteristic are those which have a strong material base—industries, armies, governments, and also churches and universities in their organizational, as opposed to their human, aspects—and these are the dominant institutions in contemporary society, both in the so-called communist and the so-called free worlds. Alienation in this sense—that is, the separation of the individual from any genuine involvement in the control of the conditions of his existence—is a prominent feature of the crisis; and it attacks the structure of value because the locus of the activity of value is precisely in the attitude of the individual to the conditions of his existence and in his interest in perpetuating or changing them.

This active employment of value is accompanied by a more passive one in which the world acts on the individual instead of the individual's acting on the world. Of course, every true action is preceded by an assessment of the state of the world, which involves an action by the world on the individual in the form of perception. In the passive case, however, perception is followed by no overt action on the individual's part; what follows from it is purely internal and can better be spoken of as enjoyment than as involvement. Here too technological advances have changed the customary relationship between the individual and the world. Mass transport and mass communication, the development of mechanical slaves on the domestic side and of automated processes on the industrial side, have increased the amount of time available for enjoyment and decreased the power of traditional means of providing it, so that boredom, the insipidity of the life of idleness, has become the characteristic mark of the affluent society. The average man, if all his wants are provided for, so that he is free from the necessity of devoting the major part of his attention to satisfying them—*really* free as few men in the history of the world have ever been—finds that significant action is a good deal harder than he expected. It might be that a society fully liberated by technology from mundane preoccupations could produce art, philosophy, and literature of a quality hitherto undreamed of, but the evidence that is so far in from the part of our society which comes closest to this ideal is not promising, and this fact must be taken account of by any theory which claims universality. It is not enough to point out that there have always been men who turned their leisure to good account—they were always in a minority, and the question is whether the majority could possibly do so.

THE RECENT HISTORY OF ETHICS. Man's security is threatened; his identity as a producer of useful work is threatened; his ability to derive satisfaction from leisure is threatened. While these pressing problems of value have been developing on the plane of daily human involvement, what have the philosophers been up to? The nineteenth century was a period of intense philosophical activity in the field of value; the utilitarians, the evolutionists, and the self-realizationists on the one hand, and Marx and his followers on the other, concerned themselves passionately with the respective systematic consequences of intellectual and material presuppositions, individual and collective action; Kierkegaard, and later Nietzsche, explored the moral and aesthetic predicament of the individual outside any system. The intellectual consequences of the scientific and technological changes described above hardly began to be felt seriously until early in the present century. But just at that time philosophy in the English-speaking world underwent a profound change, largely due to the influence of G. E. Moore, the result of which was that almost overnight it became virtually irrelevant to anything happening on the plane of daily human involvement. Philosophy elsewhere, it is true, continued to be relevant, but on the whole it was unreliable. With the exception of the version of existentialist value theory which was developed under the pressure of the German occupation of France, not much occurred in European philosophy that could be said to be an advance on the nineteenth-century concepts of value. Although philosophy frequently drew attention to the anxieties and ambiguities of the contemporary situation—much as I have done in the earlier part of this chapter—the conclusions drawn were generally too loose and melodramatic to be of much help.

THE NATURALISTIC FALLACY. Moore's contribution to philosophy was to shift professional attention from the world to language. The main concern thus became a second-order one; and although this certainly impaired the relevance of the subject to the most pressing human problems of the day, at least it provided an environment in which the reliability of philosophical argument could be worked on dispassionately and unhurriedly. The shift was therefore, from that point of view, all to the good. Philosophy requires a certain detachment if it is to be intellectually rigorous—although it may be remarked that to be detached from human concerns, and to think them uninteresting or unimportant, are two very different things; even Kant, than whom few philosophers have been more detached or more rigorous, thought that the "supreme end" of philosophy was "the happiness of all mankind."[1] But unfortunately Moore's attention to ethical language soon led him into a disastrous mistake, his exposure of the so-called "naturalistic fallacy."[2] The term "good," Moore thought, must mean *something*, but he believed himself to have shown, by a series of arguments, that it could not mean any natural property or indeed anything at all that could be made the basis of a definition for it; "good" must therefore stand for a non-natural, directly apprehended thing or property, and every attempt to define it in terms of something else must be fallacious.

I call this view disastrous because of the effect it has had on the subsequent development of ethics. First of all it made the problem of the meaning of "good" (or "right") the fundamental problem of ethics, when it is easy to see that there are terms whose meanings are much more basic. The two main traditions in ethics have been the *teleological* (from the Greek τέλος "end"), in which the stress is on ends that are good, that is, ought to be realized, and the *deontological* (from the Greek δέω "to lack" or "to bind"—hence what is required, or obligation), in which the stress is on actions that are right, that is, ought to be done. "Ought" is therefore a more fundamental concept than either "good" or "right." But further, nobody would think, or could think, that anything ought to be done or striven for unless it *mattered*; and if there is a basic ordinary-language concern in ethics

---

[1] Immanuel Kant, *Critique of Pure Reason*, tr. N. K. Smith (London: Macmillan, 1933), p. 665.

[2] G. E. Moore, *Principia Ethica* (Cambridge Univ. Press, 1903), p. 10.

it must, I am convinced, focus on the notion of *mattering* first. Moore compared "good" to "yellow"— "yellow" cannot be defined linguistically, and yet we know directly what things are yellow, and so forth—but it is clear that although it does not matter, in general, whether things are yellow or not (unless they enter somehow into situations involving value), it always matters whether they are good or not, that this is in fact part of the meaning of "good," and that it is by no means unanalyzable. To put it differently, yellow things remain yellow whether it matters or not, and the meaning of "yellow" does not depend in any way on this distinction; with "good" the situation is entirely different.

Secondly, the assumption that "good" stood for something indefinable led to the view that there was no point in trying to get at it in any indirect empirical fashion, but that it had to be intuited directly. The trouble with intuitions is that they themselves may turn out to be learned from non-philosophical sources; it is remarkable, for instance, how many of the *prima facie* duties intuited by Ross,[3] another representative of the intuitionist view, embodied principles of behavior suitable to the educated English gentleman. The greatest weakness of any philosophy which derives its raw material mainly from language is that language always reflects the social attitudes of people who use it. The analysis of language is an extremely important part of philosophical method, but its use in any branch of philosophy having to do with value requires unusual caution. Of course the intuitionists were right in insisting that all knowledge whatever must be expressed in

---

[3] W. D. Ross, *The Right and the Good* (Oxford Univ. Press, 1930).

terms that reduce, in the end, to a set of predicates referring directly to elements of immediate experience and incapable of further verbal analysis. Their mistake was to set the level at which the process of analysis reached this terminus much too high. The more complex the predicate whose meaning is to be intuited, the greater the danger of letting in concealed assumptions.

Thirdly, the doctrine of the indefinability of "good" paved the way for the positivist conclusion that since the meaning of ethical terms was so elusive and so difficult of confirmation they had no cognitive meaning at all. The *emotive* theory of Ayer[4] and Stevenson[5] held that the use of ethical language is simply the expression of attitudes; while other terms might acquire emotive meaning along with sense meaning (given by ostensive definitions) and linguistic meaning (given by verbal definitions), ethical and aesthetic terms have *only* emotive meaning, and are characteristically defined by *persuasive* definitions. "*x* is good," according to this view, means something like "I approve of *x*; do so too." This sort of analysis of the meaning of ethical terms has been superseded, in the last decades, by even more refined analyses of the structure and function of ethical language: Urmson's work on grading,[6] Hare's on the logic of commands,[7] Nowell-Smith's on the multiple functions of ethical expressions,[8] Hampshire's

---

[4] A. J. Ayer, *Language, Truth, and Logic* (London: Victor Gollancz, 1936), Chap. VI.

[5] C. L. Stevenson, *Ethics and Language* (New Haven: Yale Univ. Press, 1944).

[6] J. O. Urmson, "On Grading," *Mind*, LIX (1950), 145.

[7] R. M. Hare, *The Language of Morals* (Oxford Univ. Press, 1952).

[8] P. H. Nowell-Smith, *Ethics* (Harmondsworth: Pelican Books, 1954).

on the segmentation of language.[9] Nobody could deny that these are important contributions to philosophy, regarded as a professional activity for which, among professionals, no excuse needs to be made. But hardly anybody would claim, either, that they have anything whatever to do with the object of moral philosophy as outlined in the previous chapter.

ETHICS AS PRACTICAL REASON. It would be stretching the point to maintain that the rather parochial development of professional philosophy is a symptom of the malaise which has infected the structure of value in society at large, although it may not be entirely unfair to suggest that the choice of ethical problems tackled by philosophy in recent years may have been influenced by the overwhelming difficulty and complexity of the genuine problems of value confronting the modern world. At any rate the retirement of the greater part of philosophical concern from *those* problems has not lessened the gravity of the crisis, which may be seen as compounded of popular bewilderment and professional indifference. The foregoing account oversimplifies both, it is true; but it provides, I think, a picture of the predicament of contemporary man which is not wholly false, and an implicit criticism of contemporary philosophy which is not wholly unjustified. Already, however, there are signs that moral philosophy is returning to an earlier conception of its task as that of *practical reason*, and some recent works —for example those of Toulmin[10] and Baier[11]—have

---

[9] Stuart Hampshire, *Thought and Action* (London: Chatto and Windus, 1960).

[10] S. E. Toulmin, *The Place of Reason in Ethics* (Cambridge Univ. Press, 1950).

[11] Kurt Baier, *The Moral Point of View* (New York: Random House, 1965).

openly taken the view that ethics provides reasons for moral action, and not merely criticisms of moral judgments or analyses of moral language. This brings us back to the question posed at the end of the previous chapter, on which the utility of moral argument was said ultimately to depend. The question at this point is, not whether men *ought* to be rational, but whether they *are*. Moral argument is argument about action, not argument about argument, which is necessarily circular. (Somebody once asked Epictetus to show him that logic was necessary, to which Epictetus replied, "What kind of argument shall I use?") It is not circular to argue that men have a moral duty to press their rational capacity beyond the point at which it is operative in everyday life, to be *especially* sure about certain kinds of decision, and so on, but that is not the argument here. It must be established that there is an everyday function of reason before reason can be appealed to at all. Once that is established moral argument can go on to insist that reason should cultivate its own powers for moral ends, but the prior question must be answered first.

GROUNDS FOR CONFIDENCE IN RATIONALITY. It is here, I think, that the first direct contribution of science to ethics is to be found. The science in question is admittedly one of the more controversial sciences, but it is one which has contributed as much as any other to the current crisis, and there may be something appropriate in an appeal to it at this point. Psychoanalytic theory advances the hypothesis that the basic drives which characterize the id, under the pleasure principle, are deflected and controlled by the ego, under the reality principle; the process of ontogenesis consists in the discovery, by the ego, that the id is self-destructive when left to its own devices, and of the consequent repression or sublimation of instinctual energy in search of less primitive and immediate forms of satisfaction. Now discovery is a rational process, even when it is not fully conscious, and the fact that the reality principle is able to make any headway at all against instinct is evidence of rationality, not as something to be striven for but as something normally provided. Pain or retribution following action constitute data on which the ego constructs an argument, the outcome of which is a prescription for an altered line of action.

This is not yet conscious argument, and it is certainly not argument functioning in the solution of problems which involve choice between alternatives; the painful alternative is rejected without any pause for deliberation. In moral situations things are more complicated. Freud locates traditional morality in the superego, the internalized code of a society which has accumulated the experience of many egos and which communicates its standards by means of parental authority. But this makes morality as irrational, from the viewpoint of the individual, as instinct; the id tries to coerce the ego from within, while the superego tries to coerce it from without. And this view of morality is in agreement with the received doctrine in all ages prior to this one: original sin needs to be redeemed by transcendent grace, hence morality requires a religious warrant, and so on. The trouble is that in this "war in the members," as St. Paul calls it, the rational ego has no part to play, so that for very many people the subjective consciousness remains in utter moral perplexity, assailed in turn by libidinal drives and by automatic—that is, perfectly learned—responses of guilt.

The real root of the crisis lies here—in the fact that

society has relied so long on external standards of morality that most of its members are no longer able to formulate their own, or at least to furnish independent corroboration of other people's. The true function of moral argument, which is located, as all genuine argument must be, in the ego and not in the superego, is to enable the individual not only to follow rules but to know when not to follow them, not only to repress instincts but to know when to indulge them. The ego learns to outwit not only the id but also the superego itself. But if, in so doing, it is to remain moral, it must be guided by rational principles of a different order from that of any associated with traditional external moralities, and these principles form the subject matter of moral philosophy properly conceived.

III
The Role of Authority

PROPER AND IMPROPER USES OF AUTHORITY. So far the argument seems to be leading towards a Utopian vision of a population guided by rational principles on the basis of which its members construct moral arguments and thereby obtain ready solutions to their moral problems. It would be idle to pretend that this state of affairs could ever actually be realized. The ordinary man cannot tackle every problem by going back to principles—in fact he very rarely appeals to principles in our sense at all, what he calls his "principles" being rules of thumb to which he is emotionally attached, that is, which make him feel guilty when they are violated. These he may have acquired directly from parents or teachers, or indirectly by a kind of social osmosis; it is not unlikely that at some time or other he may have given a good deal of thought to them, but if challenged he will probably be at a loss to defend them articulately. As far as he is concerned all principles whatever, in our sense, are transcendent; he commands evidence for none of them, but accepts them, as he always has, on authority. To believe something it is enough for him if he knows that it is believed by people he respects, as long as it meets a rough intuitive test of plausibility.

But the same thing could be said, *mutatis mutandis*, of the ordinary man's knowledge of the external world. Whether in science or morality the appeal is more frequently to authority than to experience; this has always been so and it probably always will be. And yet the nature of the authority in the two cases is clearly not the same; they offer an illuminating comparison, epitomized in the contrast between the doctor and the priest. (For the purposes of argument I shall oversimplify this contrast considerably; doctors are far more vulnerable to criticism, and priests perhaps far less so, than will appear in what follows.) Both men occupy positions of virtually total authority over persons committed to their care, in the sense that, according to the principles by which they operate, the individual who questions or refuses to comply with the verdict they pronounce places his life in jeopardy, although he has as a rule no way of making an independent assessment of the accuracy of that verdict. But the proportion of the population which takes any notice at all of the verdict of the priest grows continually smaller, while everybody continues to obey the doctor.

The difference between them is a difference not only in the ground of their authority but also in the manner of its application. The ordinary man understands the ground of the doctor's authority to be experimental, and he understands, or can be brought to understand, the principles on which experimental science rests. What he cannot do, and what he is glad to pay the doctor to do for him, is work out the consequences of the body of experimental knowledge as they apply to his own condition, or even for that matter understand his condition as it must be understood if that knowledge is to be applicable to it at all. The ground of the priest's authority, on the other hand, is another authority, and so on in a chain of authority terminating in a divinely authoritative revelation of some sort or other. The application of it is by comparison with the previous case simple, and the ordinary man can generally follow the argument which leads from the goodness of God to his own sinful state. The authority of the priest is needed to reinforce the principles of religion. By contrast, the authority of the doctor is needed to ensure the rational application of the principles of medicine, which themselves require no reinforcement. That is the difference. Obedience to the doctor does not involve the individual in any abdication of his own responsibility for himself; he is simply making use of the division of specialized labor in a complex society. But obedience to the priest does involve such an abdication, even though, as Sartre has shown, it is an abdication which can never really be successful:

> But if you seek counsel—from a priest, for example—you have selected that priest; and at bottom you already knew, more or less, what he would advise. In other words, to choose an adviser is already to commit oneself by that choice.[1]

---

[1] Jean-Paul Sartre, "Existentialism Is a Humanism," in W. Kaufman, ed., *Existentialism from Dostoievsky to Sartre* (New York: Meridian Books, 1956), p. 297.

It is just this inescapable responsibility of the individual for his own behavior which makes the question of authority so crucial.

THE EMERGENCE OF SCIENCE AS AUTHORITATIVE. Moral authority has always been closer to the priest than to the doctor. It is not the intention of this book to maintain that the theory of morals can be made into a science, but it is its intention to see how nearly it can be brought to rest on elementary principles of truth and falsity, and how far it can be removed from transcendent principles of good and evil. Scientists have managed to arrive at a basis for agreement which transcends ideological, religious, and national differences, and so far theirs is the only community of genuinely international scope. They have tacitly suppressed considerations of morality, political or otherwise; the ground of their agreement is not a common understanding of what is right and wrong, but a common understanding of what is true and false. Viewed historically, this represents a remarkable inversion of the order of doubt and certainty. In some earlier periods—the late Middle Ages are a case in point—there was general agreement about right and wrong, but fierce philosophical argument about truth and falsity. Judgments of truth were held to rest on transcendent principles, and reconciliation, between Thomists and Ockhamists for example, was impossible in the absence of such principles held in common. On the practical side doctors formed a kind of priesthood, and traced their authority to Hippocrates and Galen; the alchemists looked back to the half-mythical Hermes Trismegistus, the physicists to the all too historical Aristotle. The history of science since the Middle Ages is the history of the resolution of the conflict about truth and falsity, not by the establishment of one transcendent principle rather than another, but by the elimination of such principles altogether—a step already recommended for the theory of morals in Chapter I. What happened in science was that it became clear that no principle was compelling if not assented to by individual judgment, and this made individual judgment superior to the principle. Giordano Bruno, one of the first philosophers of the new scientific attitude, puts the point bluntly in an exchange between a traditionalist and one of the moderns: when the perplexed Burchio asks, "Well, who is going to decide what the truth is?" Fracastoro replies, "That is the prerogative of every careful and wide-awake intelligence, of everybody who is as judicious and free from obstinacy as he can be. . . ."[2]

Bruno's death at the stake in 1600 showed that he was ahead of his time; such a bold reliance on one's own discernment seemed to many of his contemporaries not only blasphemous but also foolhardy, an option for relativism and chaos in preference to order and absolute assurance. This was just as true of Protestants as of Catholics, for the Reformation, while it changed the individual's relationship to authority by removing the intermediacy of the priesthood, left the *concept* of authority as it was; the warrant for the principles was now biblical rather than ecclesiastical, but that was a political change as much as a religious one. But the reliance on individual judgment for which Bruno stood, foolhardy as it may have appeared, turned out to be the condition for intellectual progress. The edifice of science has been so constructed that it rests on principles to the evaluation of which

---

[2] Quoted in G. de Santillana, ed., *The Age of Adventure* (New York: Mentor Books, 1956), p. 268.

a careful and wide-awake intelligence is entirely adequate, without on that account proving in any way unequal to its task, which is the explanation and control of nature. Of course intelligence alone did not complete the construction; imagination and evidence were also required. But the resolution that intelligence was not to be subverted by authority was worth dying for, as the evidence itself (which, as Jaspers points out in defense of Galileo, could not suffer by retraction[3]) was not.

SCIENCE AS IMAGINATION CONTROLLED BY EVIDENCE. The combination of evidence and imagination is worth further attention. All authority, unless the supernatural hypothesis is taken seriously, has its orgin in the human imagination, and science no less than religion began as a speculative account of some of the more noticeable regularities in human experience. Science dealt originally with natural, as opposed to human, events; the sciences of man, although they were anticipated by Aristotle, developed comparatively late. The province of the earliest science included the stars and the seasons, the elements, the generation and decay of plants and animals, health and disease; and the imagination of the early scientists constructed original and often extravagant accounts of the way the world must be if these things and processes are to behave as they do. Religion dealt with some of the same things, regarded however in their special capacity as determiners of human security and welfare—as needed or feared—and with other phenomena such as joy and terror, love and hatred, death and the hope of immortality, and so on. There was frequently a striking

---

[3] Karl Jaspers, *The Perennial Scope of Philosophy*, tr. R. Manheim (London: Routledge and Kegan Paul, 1950), p. 10.

similarity in the circumstances of the imaginative production of what would become a scientific theory and what would become a religious dogma: the heightened quality of some experience of intellectual conviction which led to its being taken for a vision or a revelation, the compulsion to write or recite what had been seen or revealed, often in the special literary form appropriate to stories which were to be remembered by the initiated but kept from the masses, the censoring or digesting of the esoteric doctrine for exoteric purposes. Very often, in fact, the scientific and religious elements were combined in a single traditional story, a myth whose purpose was the explanation of widely accepted beliefs about the world and about human affairs.

What distinguished the later development of science from the later development of religion was that in science the imagination was brought under control without having to be suppressed. Of course as time went on both kinds of imaginative construction began to suffer from certain limitations, not the least of which was that once a myth had been generally accepted an alternative myth stood very little chance of establishing itself unless it could be used as the emotional platform for some political change. Most of the new religions grew up in periods of political ferment. Within a particular religious tradition there was less and less room for the free exercise of the imagination, at least where the explanation of phenomena or behavior was concerned, and this may have been one of the reasons why art flourished, since it offered the main outlet for imaginative construction of a non-controversial sort. But the history of science, when it managed to disentangle itself from religion, has been the history of *imagination controlled by evidence;* and this arrangement has the great virtue that there is an acceptable procedure for the *rejection* of an earlier imaginative account, which leaves the contemporary imagination (that is, at the time of the rejection) free to replace the old account with a new one. Changes in the scientific tradition can therefore come about peaceably, as changes in the religious tradition never can.

The upshot of all this has been that science, which is seen to conduct its affairs in a reasonably open manner and to treat its principles as corrigible in the light of further evidence, has come to be very generally trusted as a guide to practical action in the physical, and to some extent in the human, world. Once again the point is oversimplified—there could be cited plenty of examples of stubbornness and prejudice among scientists, and many cases in which scientific advice turned out to be disastrous. (It has been suggested, for example, that it was not until the middle of the nineteenth century that medicine cured more people than it killed.) Such cases, however, do not detract from the general success of science in arriving at a *modus operandi* that requires no transcendent assumptions, is generally plausible, has obvious advantages, and reflects the advancement of knowledge.

A DISTINCTION BETWEEN APPLIED SCIENCE AND APPLIED MORALITY. Ordinary men, as has already been remarked, do not become involved with science directly; what in fact happens is that science is mediated to them by engineers, whose task it is to take principles (such as the generation of electricity) worked out on a small scale and apply them on a large scale, or to adapt sensitive reactions (such as those involved in photography) to processes which will work under the gross conditions of everyday use. Perhaps what the first chapter called for was a kind of moral engineering, a similar adaptation of refined philosophical principles to daily moral problems. But the analogy cannot be pushed too far. The man who uses the device provided by the engineer need have no understanding at all of the laws in virtue of which it operates; pressing the button that turns on the air conditioner—although (within the limits of the reliability of the machine) it depends on a practical knowledge of a constant physical relationship, that is, the relationship between buttons and room temperature—does not involve any acquaintance with thermodynamics; the relationship in question, from the layman's point of view, is in fact a strictly magical one, comparable in its intelligibility to the relationship between sticking pins in effigies and the suffering of one's enemies. We are certainly not looking for push-button morality. That would not count as morality at all, since for an action to be moral the agent must be at least to some extent aware of the relationship between the action and its consequences, not merely as a constant conjunction but as a case of a more general relationship between an intention and its achievement.

All this is in keeping with the difference discussed in Chapter I between the laws of science and moral rules, the former standing at a certain distance from daily experience of the world, the latter being immediately relevant to it. The logical parallel, however, need not be given up. If from the hypothetical principles of science laws may be deduced which can be trusted to apply to physical events, and which are therefore in a sense authoritative for the determination of such events, perhaps rules may be deduced from the hypothetical principles of morality which will be similarly authoritative for the determination of human actions, and obedience to which will not constitute the abdication of individual responsibility spoken of earlier in this chapter.

But if this is what is in mind, why not simply make morality a science? To answer that question some of the limitations of the scientific approach must be investigated.

IV

The Nature and Limitations of Science

THE ELEMENTS OF SCIENTIFIC THEORY. The function of science is the explanation of nature in its own terms;[1] its method is that of imagination controlled by evidence. Science *exists*, however, as a body of universal propositions believed by scientists, in the light of which particular propositions about matters of fact are rendered intelligible and seen to be coherently related to one another. Explanation is the logical relation between the universal propositions and the particular propositions, the latter following according to some (usually deductive) pattern of inference from the former when appropriate local conditions are inserted.

[1] Peter Caws, *The Philosophy of Science, A Systematic Account* (Princeton: Van Nostrand, 1965), p. 11.

(Also one universal proposition may be said to explain another if the required logical relation holds between them.)

The particular propositions about matters of fact, which form the terminus of the explanatory relation, may be called *factual descriptions*, and the sentences by means of which they are expressed may be called *protocol sentences* (the record of an experiment is sometimes called a protocol). A series of factual descriptions of a freely falling apple, for example, might be expressed in the protocol sentences:

$$t = 0, s = 0$$
$$t = \tfrac{1}{2}, s = 4$$
$$t = 1, s = 16$$

and so on (in which t is the time in seconds and s the distance fallen in feet). Such sentences are reports of individual observations; they may be extended to include sets of individual observations, but there is no such thing as a generalized protocol. Their acceptance by science depends as a rule on their being agreed upon by more than one observer; they must be *intersubjectively corroborated*, or at least able to be so in principle. Protocol sentences describe states of affairs, and the judgment that a certain state of affairs is in fact the case rests on *perception*. Perceptual data in their most primitive form may be simply impressions of heat or cold, light or darkness; the discrimination of the fine structure of the field of appearance which characterizes the observations of scientists represents a degree of sophistication which has been acquired through years of training. The rendering of what appears perceptually as a *description* calls not only for discrimination but also for the command of a language whose terms are precisely defined and apply to *classes* of perceived states of affairs, so that anybody who reads the description, although he may not have observed the state of affairs it describes, recognizes it as belonging to a class some of the members of which he has observed. (Training in science consists, among other things, in giving the student an opportunity to observe a number of paradigmatic states of affairs on the basis of which he can interpret what other scientists are talking about.) It is important for the parallel with the theory of value to realize that it is a long step from raw perceptual data to a description, and an equally long one from the ordinary man's description of some state of affairs (which will probably omit most of the relevant data) to the scientist's.

The universal propositions which constitute the main body of science (to which, strictly speaking, factual descriptions do not belong) are of two principal kinds, *generalizations* and *hypotheses*, the difference between them being that hypotheses contain terms not found in the vocabulary of description, while generalizations (which are generalizations *of* particular factual descriptions) contain only descriptive—or *observational* —terms, apart of course from grammatical or logical connectives. For example, the generalization covering the falling apple referred to above is the well-known formula:

$$s = \tfrac{1}{2}gt^2$$

(in which g is the acceleration of gravity), while the hypothesis which accounts for it is Newton's formula for gravitational attraction:

$$f = -G\frac{m_1 m_2}{r^2}$$

(in which G is the universal gravitational constant, m_1 and m_2 the masses of the attracting bodies—in this case the apple and the earth—and r the distance between their centers). f stands for a *force*, which is not observed directly but through its effect on the apple. The relation between the sentences which express hypotheses, the sentences which express generalizations, and the protocol sentences which as we saw above express factual descriptions, is as follows: protocol sentences are *instantiations* of generalizations, generalizations are *consequences* of hypotheses. Hypotheses, however, always need to be taken in sets, or to be supplemented by other sentences, before generalizations can be derived from them, since their vocabulary is not the same as that of the generalizations. The formula about the falling body follows from the universal formula only if, in addition to the necessary values for the constant of gravitation and the mass and radius of the earth, the definition known as Newton's second law:

$$f = ma$$

(in which m is the mass of a moving body and a the acceleration produced in it by a force f), is provided, since this yields the special value g for the acceleration of gravity, from which the actual distances fallen can be calculated. (This value, of course, works out at 32 feet per second. It is the same for all falling bodies near the surface of the earth because the mass of the falling body cancels out in the derivation.)

Generalizations and hypotheses are so called because they have a certain logical form and a certain relation to protocol sentences, not because they are true. Generalizations which have been shown to the satisfaction of scientists to be true—that is, which have been *accepted* as such—are called *laws*, and in a similar way hypotheses which satisfy this condition are sometimes called *principles*. But showing truth in the two cases involves two different sets of considerations. To revert to the example given above: one of the generalizations implicit in it is that whenever a heavy object is released from rest and allowed to fall freely near the surface of the earth its acceleration will be g. The trouble with establishing the truth of this is that most heavy bodies in the universe never have been, never will be, and indeed never could be released from rest and allowed to fall freely near the surface of the earth, so that to assert what *would* happen if they *were* so released (which is what the generalization amounts to) goes far beyond the evidence, which is merely an accumulation of protocol sentences like the one given. This is a logical pitfall from which there is no satisfactory escape, but philosophers have often skirted round it by appealing to transcendent principles like the Principle of the Uniformity of Nature. All that is required to escape this difficulty is to admit that the generalization cannot be finally known to be true, but to resolve to accept it as true until evidence presents itself to the contrary. By our definition of "law" this is to admit the generalization as a law; and certainly a sufficient number of observations of heavy objects actually accelerating at the required rate predisposes the observer, in the absence of contrary instances, to accept such a law.

Universal forces, on the other hand, are never observed; the hypothesis always says: "If the world were constructed in such and such a way, and if there were such and such a relation between its construction and its behavior, such and such behavior would be observed; it *is* observed, therefore it is likely that the world is in fact constructed in that way." The problem is to know when this likelihood is great enough to justify the acceptance of the hypothesis as true. The answer is that it is never finally great enough, but that the coherence of the sentences derived from the hypotheses with sentences generalized from the protocol, and their usefulness in prediction, enable us to make a resolve similar to the one for laws: we hang on to our principles until the evidence compels us to change them. The nature of the evidence which would compel such a change is not as obvious for principles, however, as it is for laws. The refutation of a law involves the observation of factual situations which are directly incompatible with it—heavy objects remaining suspended in mid-air, for example. But a principle may be refuted by its being shown that after all the law does not follow from it, without the emergence of any new evidence; or, on the other hand, new evidence may not refute it if it can be shown that the amended law can also be made to follow from it with suitable adjustments in other parts of the theory.

THE RELEVANCE OF THEORY TO THE WORLD. The existence of a theory, complete with principles and laws, enables the scientist to make assertions which seem to the ordinary man quite implausible in the light of his own experience. The scientist may say, for example, that electromagnetic waves and other forms of radiation are constantly passing through the ordinary man's body, that chairs and tables are composed of tiny particles in violent motion, and so on. The scientist starts out with observations not much more complex than those that other people make, but when fed into theories his observations lead to conclusions apparently at variance with the plain evidence of the senses. Nobody would tolerate this state of affairs if it were not for the fact that entertaining such hypotheses makes it possible to predict what the plain evidence of the senses will be at some future time—a feat which, apart from its obvious usefulness, is impressive enough to render all sorts of eccentricities perfectly acceptable. In most cases the prediction is a good deal less than perfect and its outcome is highly probable rather than fully certain, but since this probability is usually computable with some accuracy it is known how much reliance can wisely be placed on the prediction, and this is the next best thing to certainty.

One of the great puzzles of the philosophy of science has always been the *origin* of the hypotheses which, by standing apart from experience, enable thought to leave the plane of experience and return to it elsewhere or in the future. One popular view has been that the hypotheses are arrived at by *induction* from particular experiences, but this is clearly inadequate, since, as we have seen, hypotheses make reference to things which are not encountered in experience. Obviously hypotheses must rest in *some* way on experience, but they cannot do so in the simple inductive way. The most satisfactory account makes them the products of the scientific imagination; in Peirce's words they are "the spontaneous conjectures of instinctive reason." [2] Reason does not make its conjectures at random, however; there is an intuitive notion of *relevance* to experience which can be formalized in logical terms by means of the set of relationships between protocol sentences, generalizations, and hypotheses given above. Hypotheses, when formulated, are seen to have some potential connection with experience through their joint logical consequences. Whether these consequences, when

---

[2] C. S. Peirce, "A Neglected Argument for the Reality of God," in P. P. Wiener, ed., *Values in a Universe of Chance, Selected Writings of Charles S. Peirce* (New York: Doubleday Anchor Books, 1958), p. 371.

worked out in detail, will be *correct* descriptions of experience remains to be seen (if they are not, the hypotheses need modification). But they will certainly be descriptions of some *possible* experience.

The logical connections between hypotheses and protocol sentences, and those between one protocol sentence and another, by means of which predictions are made, are assumed to reflect in some way causal connections between the things to which the sentences refer. With respect to the first case, unobservable events (for example, quantum transitions) must, if science is to have any standing at all as an account of the real world, play a part in the causal determination of observable ones (for example, the emission of light). With respect to the second, a prediction is a logical movement, via the theory, from a set of protocol sentences describing events previously observed (the *data*) to a protocol sentence describing the predicted event; and if the prediction is to be useful this movement must anticipate the causal movement, via the physical world, from the events previously observed to the predicted event. This assumption of parallelism between the logical structure of theory and the causal structure of the world is itself a meta-scientific hypothesis whose confirmation is provided in a rough way by the success of science in making predictions. But we would know nothing of the causal structure, and could not begin to construct a theory, if we were not somehow involved in the physical world —if in fact we did not have bodies equipped with sense organs. The perceptions on the basis of which we enunciate protocol sentences are themselves the end points of causal chains.

Figure 1 shows how causality enters into the picture in a dual sense. The unbroken arrows in the diagram represent causal connections, and their direction makes an important point. If *A* is the cause of *B*, *B* cannot be the cause of *A;* and furthermore, according to the standard analysis of causality, if *A* is the cause of *B*, *A* must *precede* *B* in time. The causal process is unidirectional. Since, however, the perception of *A*, on

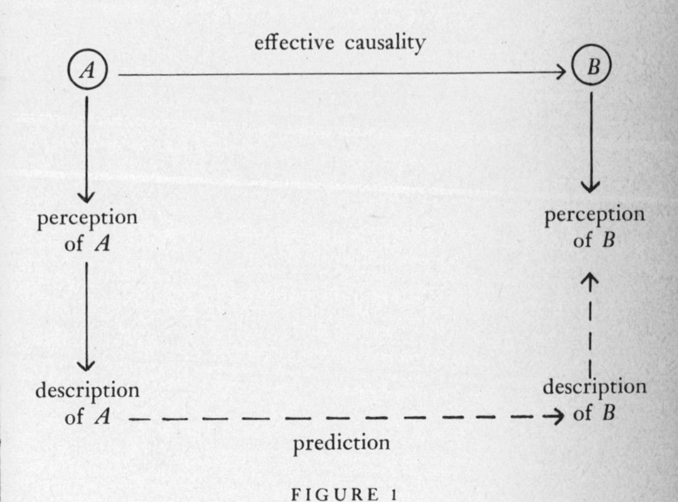

FIGURE 1

which knowledge of *A* rests, is in some way a causal consequence of *A* itself, it follows that *knowledge is always retrospective.* An event cannot be described until it has happened, strictly speaking—that is, an eyewitness account cannot be given. Prediction, although it is apparently a counterexample of this point, is not the same as knowledge; the broken line in the diagram, which leads from the description of *A* to the description of *B*, and which must produce the latter before *B* happens if it is to represent a prediction, is broken because there is always an element of doubt about the outcome until it is confirmed by the actual occurrence of *B*. The description and the perception confront one another, and it cannot be *known* that they will agree until the comparison is actually made. The anticipation of nature is always hypothetical and cannot be otherwise; this was a point which Hume emphasized again and again. But time continually passes; and as predictions continue to be fulfilled, our confidence in science increases. There is no logical reason why it should, but confidence is a psychological concept in any case.

THE ANALOGY BETWEEN SCIENCE AND THE THEORY OF VALUE. Science, then, while it can provide us with certain knowledge neither of the underlying and unobservable structure of the world which surrounds us nor of the future course of events, does organize such knowledge as we have in the way most likely to be useful in dealing with future contingencies; it makes the most of the situation of men of finite intelligence and powers, so that their judgments about matters of fact in everyday life can be informed and rational. Judgments of value, on the other hand, are still largely *ad hoc* or based on authority or prejudice. The task then is to learn what can be learned from the experience of science as it applies to the theory of value, and the first step is clearly to look for analogues, in the theory of value, for the various elements listed above as indispensable to the structure of science: perceptual data, protocol sentences, generalizations and laws, hypotheses and principles, together with the logical relations which link these elements and the causal relations which these links reflect. Such analogues can be found, but their character is such that it proves to be impossible to transfer the logical structure of science to the theory of value in a simple-minded way.

To start at the most elementary level, what statements about value correspond to protocol sentences? Protocol sentences express factual descriptions, and we might at first be tempted to make the empirical basis of value theory a set of such sentences describing attitudes or preferences: "*x* reports that he prefers *P* to *Q*." But this is just an ordinary protocol sentence, and does not have the special character of the theory of value. On the basis of such sentences there might be constructed a science of preferential behavior, which would be a legitimate part of psychology; it would be a scientific theory about what people actually do, or say, or think (that is, say they think) in situations appropriately described by value terms, but it would not be a theory of value. The trouble with such theories is that the scientist is always looking at someone else—"*x*"—and treating him as a datum. The physicist does not say: "*x* reports that *A* is a *B*"; he reports that *A* is a *B*, and there is all the difference in the world between the two activities. If we get rid of the intermediary and ask what kind of value sentences we enunciate about the world, which have the same particularity and immediacy and privacy as protocol sentences—for until the scientist enunciates the protocol sentence nobody but himself knows what it is going to say—I think we have to conclude that they are sentences which express, not factual *descriptions*, but factual *prescriptions*. Before the psychologist can *report* his preference of *P* to *Q*, *x* has to *prefer* *P* to *Q*; and unless he is making a deliberate effort at detachment (making a psychological report about himself), he will not just express his preference in comparative terms but will make an assertion of a quite different kind. Suppose that *P* stands for the state of affairs in which *A* is *B*, *Q* for some other (perhaps the actual) state of affairs. If *A*'s being *B* is a value for *x*, he will certainly prefer *P* to *Q*, but what matters to him is that *P* should be the case, not that he prefers it to *Q*. The paradigm of a factual prescription is "*A should be B*" or "*A ought to be B*"—"he ought not to drink so much," "you ought to protest against the war," "she should have told me the truth." These ordinary language expressions refer to states of the world, not to states of the agent's mind, which is why "I wish that *A* were *B*" or even "Would that *A* were *B*!" are unsuitable formulations. What the new expressions say about the world, however, is not empirical in the ordinary sense. They could be brought into standard form to make them more like the protocol sentences of science, but there would be a fundamental difference between the two types even so, which leads me to call the new examples *virtual protocol sentences.*

The difference is that in the expressions involving value, *the facts to which the sentences refer need not be the case.* Value attaches to his abstention, your protest, her truthfulness, whereas in fact he is an alcoholic, you acquiesce in an unjust foreign policy, she lied. These facts, however, form an essential part of the situation; the sentences are therefore complex—they have, to borrow an expression from mathematics, a real part and an imaginary or virtual part, or, in the language of this chapter, a descriptive part and a prescriptive part. In mathematics complex numbers are expressed as pairs, for example,

$$x + iy,$$

where x and y are real numbers but the i prefixed to y indicates that it enters into the expression with a special modality (i stands for $\sqrt{-1}$, so that $(iy)^2 = -(y^2)$, although there is no real solution to any equation of the form $a^2 = -b$). In the theory of value, in a somewhat analogous way, the virtual protocol sentence asserts, by implication, that something is the case and, explicitly, that something (usually, although not necessarily, something different) ought to be the case. The prefixes "it is the case that," and so forth, can be employed as a standard form, rather as Prior[3] employs them in his logic of tenses. The standard form of a straightforward protocol sentence will be "it is the case that x," while the standard form of a virtual protocol sentence will be "it is the case that x, and it ought to be the case that y." If we take x in the straightforward way to stand for "it is the case that x," and borrow i (for "imperative") as a modal prefix, so that iy stands for "it ought to be the case that y," the standard form will again be

$$x + iy.$$

The mathematical analogy is not, of course, to be taken seriously; its force is only to serve as a reminder that certain ideas cannot be expressed in simple form even when part of what is involved in them has a simple customary expression.

Although the possibility is allowed for that x and y may be identical (there is nothing inconsistent about $x + ix$), or in other words that things may be all right as they are, y always has a different temporal reference from x. *It is always future.* Even in constructions like "it ought to have been the case that y" this rule holds; there is a shift in the point of reference to a time at

---

[3] A. N. Prior, *Changes in Events and Changes in Things* (Lawrence, Kansas: Department of Philosophy, Univ. of Kansas, 1962).

which *y* was future, and the sentence translates into "it was the case that it ought to be the case that *y*," to borrow Prior's technique once more. And this difference lies at the root of the distinction between science and the theory of value. Science is a kind of knowledge, and as such it must, as was remarked above, always be retrospective. But values are different from knowledge; they do not come to us from the world, but they go from us to the world; they refer not to what is or was the case, but to what will or may be the case. They are, therefore, always *prospective* or *future referential*. The difference between science and the theory of value turns out to be as fundamental as the difference between past and future. This being so it is not surprising to find that values are not easy to discover in the world with which science deals, a fact which has disturbed a good many people in search of a science of value. They are not easy to discover because they are not yet there.

This point cannot be stressed too strongly, and it will be referred to again. For the moment we may complete the list of analogies. Principles have already been dealt with; they are just as hypothetical in the theory of value as they are in science, and their origin too is to be found in the human imagination, not elsewhere. The principles required for the system of this book will be introduced as they become relevant. Since principles of the theory of value are to lead, eventually, to prescriptions for action, their validation will follow a different pattern from the validation of scientific principles. In science we say: if the world operated according to such and such principles, such and such phenomena would be observed. To validate the principles, we ask whether the phenomena are in fact observed; if they are, that constitutes *prima facie* evidence that the principles are true. In the theory of value, on the other hand, we say: if such and such principles were acted upon, such and such a world would result. To validate these principles we ask, not only whether such a world really *would* result, but also whether this is the kind of world we want; if it is, that constitutes *prima facie* evidence that the principles are right.

Laws in science correspond to *rules* in value theory; the rules have the same amphibian nature as the laws, being on the one hand acceptable generalizations of virtual protocol sentences and on the other the deductive consequences of hypothetical principles. The difference between rules and laws is like the difference between virtual protocol sentences and straightforward ones, in that rules look like laws with an imperative modal prefix (which must also be attached to at least one of the principles from which the rule is derived). It is to be noted that the descriptive part of the virtual protocol sentence drops out on generalizing, since there may be indefinitely many states of affairs x in which we may wish to assert that it ought to be the case that y—including, as we have seen, the case in which x and y are identical. The point of having a descriptive part there at all is that it makes a difference in the application of the rule. If x is identical with y, obviously no action is called for by the rule; if not, the action called for depends on the relation between x and y. The logical relations between principles, rules, and prescriptions are then strictly analogous to those between principles, laws, and descriptions in science; the relations hold between the indicative contents of the sentences in question, and the modal prefix is carried through unchanged.

A PHENOMENOLOGICAL DISTINCTION: KNOWING AND

WILLING. The chief difficulty with this scheme of analogies[4] arises at the level in the theory of value corresponding to raw perceptual data in scientific theory. What, on the side of value, corresponds to seeing blue or hearing a loud noise? Here it seems to me useful to revive a classical usage in philosophy and speak of *conation* as an analogue of perception. *Conatus*, in Spinoza,[5] is "the effort by which each thing endeavors to persevere in its own being"; it therefore has the required direction towards the future which we have identified as the fundamental characteristic of value. By "conative data" I shall mean the intuitively felt tendencies of an individual to accept some things or circumstances and reject others, to try to acquire some and to try to get rid of others. "Data" is perhaps misleading, but is worth keeping for the analogy. I do not mean that one discovers such tendencies in oneself and makes the *fact* that they are there the basis for prescriptive utterances; the tendencies themselves are the basis. But the rendering of the tendencies as an articulate prescription calls for the same degree of experience and sophistication as is required for the rendering of raw perceptual data as an articulate description.

The point here is that the relation of man to the world is not only a static relation of knowledge but also a dynamic relation of will, and that science is equipped to deal only with the former. The way in which values are constituted out of conations requires

---

[4] The scheme of analogies is shown diagrammatically in Table 1. The term "nomological" (from the Greek νόμος, "law") covers cases of empirical regularity; the rest of the diagram is self-explanatory.

[5] Benedict de Spinoza, *Ethics*, tr. J. Gutmann (New York: Hafner, 1949), p. 135. This is Part III, Proposition VII; "effort" is a translation of "*conatus*."

TABLE 1

The Analogy Between Science and the Theory of Value

Levels	*Types of Sentence*	*Elements of Scientific Theory*	*Elements of Theory of Value*
Theoretical	hypothesis	principle	principle
Nomological	generalization	law	rule
Descriptive	observation sentence	protocol sentence	virtual protocol sentence
Phenomenological	—	perceptual data	conative data

a great deal of further analysis; once again, however, something may be learned from the way in which facts are constituted out of perceptions. The ordinary man who takes advantage of the results of scientific theory may have an imperfect understanding of the nature of fact, but in a rough and approximate fashion he knows a fact when he sees one and does not suppose that facts exist in some queer way apart from the objects and events which constitute them. But values are often thought to be a special kind of entity which might be found embedded in the world—having been put there, perhaps, by God—if only one knew where to look. One of the most celebrated of these hidden values is "meaning," for which people are endlessly searching, as though they expected it to turn up one day, whole and perfect and recognizable, putting everything in perspective and making the course of future action clear and attainable. As long as this kind of confusion persists, no theory of value can provide the rational control of man's aesthetic and moral circumstances which science provides for his material circumstances. What the theory applies to must be clearly understood, and not only in technical terms but in its everyday embodiment.

V

Fact and Value

THE TEMPORAL ASYMMETRY OF FACT AND VALUE. Fact looks to the past, value to the future; that is the fundamental difference between them. But—and here I am not merely playing games with language—they meet in the present, and not in *any* present arbitrarily selected as a point on the continuum of time but in *this* present, which divides what is already part of my cumulative experience from all the future possibilities which await me. This egocentricity is completely unavoidable. All knowledge is somebody's knowledge, every value is somebody's value, but my world is circumscribed by my knowledge, and my action in that world is determined by my values. My being as a knower and as an agent, furthermore, is located here and now, at a point in space and time on which the whole past of the universe converges and from which its whole future takes its origin. Certain elements of that future—in fact most of it—will of course be determined by causal processes which do not pass through me; I shall always be surrounded by a world over which I have little or no control. But my agency, if I really am an agent, will affect the future course of things to some degree, and make the world as a whole different from what it would have been without me.

We have seen that knowledge is the result of a causal process, and it is clear that action is in some sense the beginning of another such process, at least an apparent beginning. A crucial question, which must sooner or later be faced, is whether processes which do pass through me en route from past to future are fully causal or not, whether action really is the causal beginning of something, whether in fact I am an agent. A negative answer to that question, while it does not affect the temporal asymmetry discussed above, changes the relationship between fact and value so that it no longer depends on the asymmetry except in an academic way. According to such a view, facts, whether past or future, are what they are, while values are merely attitudes towards them adopted by an impotent subjectivity. The future differs from the past in one respect only, namely that we do not yet know it and can therefore entertain hopes and fears with respect to it and thus invest it with a kind of value. But the values we hold cannot affect the outcome of the causal process. This point has nothing to do with the issue between chance and determinism. Even the most accurate predictions in a fully determined universe suffer from practical limitations which prevent their ever being complete, and from the point of view of the individual it makes very little difference whether the source of his ignorance is contingent, as in this case, or necessary, as it would be in a universe in which chance played a part.

One of the difficulties with values as mere attitudes is that they become factual, in their own way, as soon as they are reflected upon. The advice of the Stoics (and of Descartes, who makes it one of his provisional maxims in the *Discourse on Method*) is "change your desires rather than the order of the world," but many people find that the order of the world is a good deal easier to change than their desires are, and what passes for a change of desire is often a modest rearrangement of the order of the world which removes the stimulus of desire—retreating into a monastery, for example. Desires are part of the order of the world, and the fact that they belong to an interior world makes them if anything harder to manipulate than otherwise. A regress is possible, of course: I observe the state of the world, which I cannot change; I find in myself a certain attitude towards it, let us say of discontent; at the same time I find myself taking up a second-order attitude, perhaps of disapproval, to my attitude of discontent, and so on. But these successive levels are all factual: that is the way the world is, this is the way I am. Value involves, I think, at least the potentiality of *choice*, and it therefore attaches much more plausibly to future states of the world than to states of my mind. *A value is a future fact*, selected from among a set of alternative, and mutually exclusive, future facts, and marked with an imperative. The chosen fact may not come about; in such a case we speak of the value as unrealized.

At first sight it might seem more in accord with ordinary usage to identify value with some *characteristic* of the future fact, in virtue of which it is marked with an imperative. We speak of pleasure, beauty, honor, and so on as values, and consider that these abstract qualities confer value on the facts in which they are embodied. But this puts the cart before the horse. We would not know that the abstract qualities were values if we had not first attached value to their concrete embodiments. Pleasurable experiences, beautiful objects, honorable actions constitute the empirical basis for generalizations about pleasure, beauty, and honor, and we know them for what they are without the generalizations. Also the generalizations have exceptions, which is one of the reasons why theories of value developed at the abstract level so often appear irrelevant to the experience of value in everyday life. It seems wise to begin with the unit of value in experience, namely the future fact itself, rather than with a conventional abstraction.

THE CONCEPT OF THE OPEN FUTURE. The use of the term "future" in this connection requires some clarification. In ordinary language the term automatically connotes a certain contingency, so that it is not necessary to insist that future facts are only probable. Philosophers are less tolerant; it may be argued that when I say "future fact" I mean "fact which will be the case," and that if I really mean "fact which may or may not be the case," I ought to say "possible fact." I do not wish to become involved in an argument about subjunctives, but there are two reasons why "possible" will not do: first, "possible fact" can mean "fact which may now be the case although it is not known to be," or "fact which might now be the case although it happens not to be," neither of which allows the fact as a value; second, people may very well attach value to impossible facts, as will appear later. The objection to "future" rests in part on a metaphysical assumption about determinism, from which it follows that future facts exist, implicitly, in present ones. This assumption is inconsistent with the view (developed in the next chapter) that the conscious subject plays a really efficacious role in the determination of events, and is therefore rejected. The alternative to it is to assume that statements about the future cannot now be said either to be true or to be false, which, while it is slightly awkward for logic, is in no way inconsistent with the ordinary use of future-referential statements. There is, as Aristotle insisted, a significant difference between these two assertions:

(1) It is the case that either x will happen or x will not happen.
(2) Either it is the case that x will happen or it is the case that x will not happen.

The latter pins down future facts now; the former leaves them open in the sense required by the proposed definition of value.

DIFFICULTIES IN THE ELIMINATION OF SUBJECTIVITY. While, however, the contrast between past and future is the basic element in the distinction between fact and value, it is certainly too simple-minded to do justice to the distinction as it affects our daily experience. The present, after all, is not a simple cut on the continuum of time which serves no other purpose than to separate the past from the future; it has an internal structure of its own in which fact and value overlap. What we are prepared to recognize as fact depends to a large extent on the values we hold: the way we perceive the world to be is at least in part a function of the way we would like it to be. Now science has virtually eliminated this element of subjectivity from its description of the world by its insistence on *intersubjectivity* in its protocol sentences. It is never possible to say that the world finally *is* a certain way—*saying* introduces a possibility of error which cannot ultimately be averted, and requires a vocabulary already colored by theory—but the evidence from some centuries of scientific experience suggests that normal observers under normal conditions can reach a high degree of concurrence in their reports, and this leaves open the possibility that what we all intuitively believe may be true, namely, that there may be an objective and enduring reality whose structure is reflected accurately, if not completely, in scientific theory. It would be very satisfactory if some means could be found of eliminating subjectivity from value judgments by similar techniques—for example, by insisting on intersubjective corroboration for assertions that the world *ought* to be a certain way. As a rule it is possible to find another person to agree with any imperative anybody may formulate. But the evidence from centuries of dispute about value suggests that in most cases it is at least equally easy to find somebody who disagrees, and this lends no support at all to the view that the world objectively ought to be a certain way. Facts coerce us, and there is no point in flying in the face of them; even if cherished values make us reluctant to admit that such and such is the case, we can generally be convinced by the evidence of independent observers. (In this way people discover that they are color-blind, tone-deaf, and so forth.) Independent observers are no good, though, when it comes to most questions of value. We would all admit that a lone dissenter who insisted that a course of action was wrong when everybody else said it was right would exhibit a kind of human dignity, whereas somebody who insisted that something was green when everybody else said it was blue would merely look silly.

Apart from insane persons, then, everybody can in principle be brought into a community of agreement about matters of fact, provided there is sufficient evidence, and so on. What would be needed to create a similar community of agreement for judgments of value? Evidence will not do, at least not by itself; if there is to be such a community of agreement it must, as has already been indicated, be constructed on a basis of argument. That is why the problem of value is at bottom a philosophical one while the problem of fact is at bottom a scientific one. The resolution of a scientific disagreement always rests, in the end, on evidence; the resolution of a philosophical disagreement always rests, in the end, on argument. This distinction also is too clear-cut, since scientists argue and philosophers cite cases, but I think it embodies the main point of difference. Science consists of the accumulation and explanation of evidence about the past, with all that that implies for our knowledge of the future; the theory of value consists of the formulation and justification of arguments about the future, with all that that implies for our attitude toward the past. The apparent future reference of science, in prediction, involves a hypothetical shift of perspective to a point from which the predicted event is seen as past; the apparent reference of value to the past, in approval or regret, involves a hypothetical shift of perspective to a point from which the approved or regretted event is seen as future. "In his circumstances I would have done the same thing" is a form of approbation which puts the speaker temporarily in a position where the decision is yet to be taken; "if I had known then what I know now, I would never have done it" is to be construed in a similar way. Past actions or events are not approved or regretted as facts merely, but as facts *which might have been otherwise.*

If this shift of perspective seems to introduce an intolerable distortion into the ordinary meaning of "regret" and "approval," there may be allowed to be such things as mere attitudes—for example, of horror at the behavior of Hitler—into which value clearly enters and to which an emotive analysis would be adequate. Even here it seems to me that the horror lies in the fact that at some point in the past the "final solution" had *not yet* been decided upon and that the decision was an apparently free choice of an apparently human being. But granting a present feeling of (perhaps retrospective) moral or aesthetic disapproval of a past fact, with no future-referential component at all, not even a displaced one, it must be admitted that the role of value in this feeling is merely passive, except as it is accompanied by a resolve not to let the same thing happen again. In the absence of such a resolve, in fact, we often use expressions like "pious horror," as an indication that in some way the attitude is not to be taken seriously. The object of this book is the clarification of moral judgment as *active*, that is, as contributing to the determination of action on the part of the person making the judgment; from this point of view the detached assessment of the actions of others, the debate about what should be *called* "good" or "right" after the fact, about what "virtue" means, and so on, is of secondary interest merely. What is important is what men decide to do, the process by which they arrive at the decision, and the arguments which enter into the process. It is only in this area that value has its full significance.

THEORY AS THE RECTIFICATION OF EXPERIENCE. About some imperatives—for example, food and drink for people at the extremes of hunger and thirst, or relief for those in extreme pain—there can be no argument, and this is liable to lead to a serious confusion, which is at the root of all hedonistic theories of value. On the most primitive level conative tendencies are indeed factual and inescapable; there is no choice in the matter. But these overriding tendencies, instilled by the evolutionary process as necessities of survival, have no more to do with the theory of value than certain mechanisms of perception with a similar origin, such as the dilation and contraction of the pupil of the eye, have to do with the theory of knowledge. They are not activities consciously engaged in, even though the conscious activities of knowing and valuing depend on them or on processes like them. Valuing bears to such raw feeling rather the relationship that knowing bears to untrained seeing; just as science must be suspicious of what is superficially seen, such as moving stars and bent sticks, so also the theory of value must be suspicious of what is superficially felt, such as a desire for pleasure and a dislike of pain. The function of the theory is precisely to render the intellect independent of ephemeral considerations like these, to rectify experience by making it possible to move away from the immediacy of experience in thought, and to bring the outcome of this thought to bear on future experience. Naive perception comes to naive conclusions about the world; science starts from the fact that we have some knowledge, even if it is crude, and goes on to determine as best it can what we really know and do not know. Naive conation, in a similar way, comes to naive conclusions about action; the theory of value starts from the fact that we have some desires, even if they are clumsy, and goes on to determine as best it can what we really want and do not want. The community of agreement for which we are seeking comes about only if individual values are rectified by a theory of value held in common.

FACTS AS VALUES, VALUES AS FACTS. There are four special cases of the interaction of fact and value which may help clarify the relation between them. First of all, *facts may be regarded as values*—for example, in the pursuit of historical or scientific truth. The search for evidence about the past is really an attempt to arrive at a future state of fuller knowledge of the past; the search for scientific law is an attempt to bring about conditions, again in the future, in which man's understanding of or control over his world will be greater than it is now. It has been rightly insisted upon, by a great number of recent commentators, that science cannot be considered coldly objective, by contrast for example with literature or the arts. If it had not engaged men's passions, they would never have invented it. (At the same time it must be remembered that science requires a disciplined separation of the values it serves from the objects it studies.)

Secondly, *values may be regarded as facts*. There are two senses in which this relationship may be understood: the first, which is classical, coincides closely with the analysis given above, while the second, which is modern, exhibits a confusion which has already been criticized. For Plato the highest value resides in a real object which really exists and is therefore fully factual, namely the Form of the Good; for Aristotle the highest good is that to which the universe tends, whose actualization is the goal of every rational activity, including the activities of nature itself. The value-laden character of fact is clear, especially in the works of Plato, for whom knowledge is *better* than opinion —not, it is true, knowledge of a merely factual kind (for example, of the fact that Athens is to the east of

Syracuse), but of a special sort of fact (for example, of the fact that man's relationship to the world is such and such).

The second sense in which values may be regarded as factual is that of the social scientist, and it is of comparatively recent origin. The values which men hold determine their behavior, at least insofar as that behavior is determined by them at all, and it is therefore easy to suppose that a science of behavior is the only true science of value. Accordingly, analyses of preference and of choice are offered as guides to the nature of value. If introspective accounts are to be ruled out as inherently untrustworthy, then the only way to find out about values is to observe preferences. The thesis of behaviorism brings everything into the realm of science by insisting that it should be looked at only from the outside. If what one wants is a scientific account, then this is perfectly proper and indeed unavoidable; and since the only sensible thing for rational beings to do, if they are trying to explain events, is to follow the methods of science as far as they can be pushed, behaviorism needs to make no excuses for itself. But part of the purpose of this book is to see whether there are aspects of value for which a scientific account is inadequate; and the assumption that preferences actually expressed in actions are straightforward reflections of values actually held is much too simple. Preference involves a choice between actual alternatives, and it very often happens that these do not include the valued alternative at all. This does not mean that no preference will be expressed. The strongest desire that a given state of affairs should come about is wholly compatible with the realization that it will never do so, and in such a situation behavior, whether action or description—for example, in an interview—may not provide any clues at all to the values involved. Without data the scientist is lost, and gross changes may take place in values without any change in the data for anybody except the person whose subjectivity is the locus of the values in question. Such a dissonance between value and preferential behavior might lead to a charge of bad faith against the person concerned, but that is no excuse for behavioristic oversimplification.

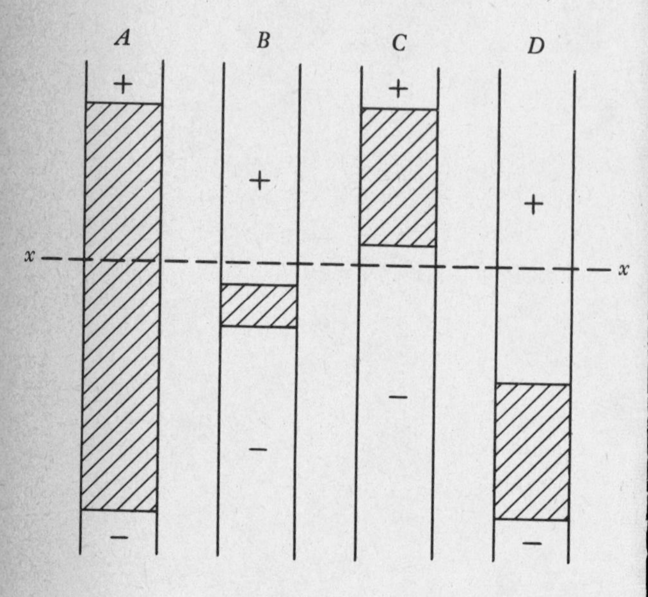

FIGURE 2

Further, even if in the individual case expressed preferences reflect values accurately, disagreement can still arise between individuals in a way which is unknown in the case of perception. Figure 2 shows schematically a number of different ways in which preferential behavior, and hence value, may occur in individual persons. The shaded area I call the *range of indifference*, the area above it marked "+" I call the *range of positive value*, and the area below it marked "−" the *range of negative value*. The individual *A* is one to whom nothing matters very much; he has a wide range of indifference flanked by very narrow ranges of value. *B*, on the other hand, is extremely sensitive to everything, so that for him the reverse is true. *C* is hypercritical and *D* too easily satisfied, to put the matter in the crudest terms; their ranges are therefore skewed. The event *x*, represented by a broken line crossing all four individuals, does not matter at all to *A*; it has a negative value for *C*, but a positive one for *B* and *D*. Agreement is therefore impossible. All this is not to be taken as meaning, however, that social scientists are wasting their time. Science does what it must, that is, it engages in the search for regularities in experience and for theories to account for them. Values may, and indeed must, enter into the explanation of human behavior, and if there were no other analytical approach to them they might take their place alongside electromagnetic and gravitational fields as theoretical entities required for the systematic completion of the sciences of man, as fields are required for the completion of the science of nature. But it is quite clear that the matter need not end there, and that we have access to the structure of value in a much more direct way than that in which we have access to the structure of the physical world.

FACTS AS INADEQUATE TO VALUES. The two relationships between fact and value so far dealt with tend, if anything, to confuse fact with value, by showing that facts may be made the object of concern and that values may enter into the scientific explanation of facts. The confusion is only apparent, and it has been shown that the distinction can be preserved even in these cases. There are two other relationships which have the effect rather of sharpening the contrast. First, *facts by themselves always fall short of value.* This is seen most clearly in the literature of boredom and has already been spoken of in Chapter II. The contemplation of fact as fact can, it is true, produce a certain kind of satisfaction, but the satisfaction is not so much in the fact's being what it is as in its being known or having been successfully established. Satisfaction, again, cannot be equated with value—it represents the enjoyment of value, but the value is *what is enjoyed,* not the enjoyment of it. Satisfaction arises from the realization of a state of the world to which an imperative has been attached. Facts must therefore *have been* future for somebody, at least implicitly, if they are to count as values. (An unanticipated fact may be a value if it is such that an imperative would have been attached to it had it been thought of before the event; also the fact that it *was* unanticipated may be a value—consider, for example, the disappointment of a child who says "I wanted it to be a surprise.") The facts themselves, apart from these modalities, lack any value whatever. This by now is almost tautologous, and yet it is profoundly significant for an understanding of the special flatness which characterizes lives full of material possessions but without imagination and without hope. The understanding of the factual situation helps, but it may not be enough by itself to remove a sense of incompleteness and dissatisfaction—there must be some participation in the emergence of new facts, a sense of involvement in the situation as something more than a mere onlooker. The story of Socrates' disappointment with the philosophy of Anaxagoras is well known: Anaxagoras talked about *nous*, or mind, as the principle according to which the world moves purposively from one state to another, but when it came to explaining particular facts he forgot all about *nous* and referred instead only to "air, and ether, and water and other eccentricities." Socrates insisted that what gave direction to his actions was his conception of what was best, and this in a very concrete form—namely, his determination to stay in Athens and endure the punishment the state was to inflict. (The passage occurs in the *Phaedo*, just before Socrates' death, and he is explaining why he has not run away.) Obviously action requires an antecedent factual basis, but it is not to be explained fully in terms of factual antecedents; that at least is Socrates' contention. Facts, once they have transpired, die and become immortal, and at this point they cease to be relevant to the determination of future facts, which is the province of action and therefore of value.

VALUES AS OUTREACHING FACTS. The inverse of this relationship is provided by the very simple observation that *value always goes beyond any fact or set of facts* which may have been established. In order to act it is never enough simply to take account of the state of affairs; there must always be a commitment to the securing of that state of affairs against change or to the realization of a new state of affairs. The literature of *ennui* is complemented by the literature of the *engagé*; the first poses the problem to which the second offers the answer. It is necessary for a man to involve himself, to become engaged in some project, to make the leap of faith. Religious faith, in the West, has been on the whole a poor illustration of the concept, but in Kierkegaard the idea is explicit: it is the election of a future state of the world which is by no means likely to come about in the ordinary course of events and the attachment to it of the imperative. In this way the whole situation comes alive; there may be anguish, dread, fear and trembling, but there will not be boredom. Faith is an extreme version of the situation of value, in which the stakes are high and the possibility of failure correspondingly great. Kierkegaard himself could not attain to it, he says—he was not the Knight of Faith but the Knight of Infinite Resignation, who saw the hopelessness of what he had chosen as a value.[1] It is not necessary to conduct one's life in terms quite as melodramatic as Kierkegaard's, but without some degree of this commitment to the chosen value it is not truly constituted as a value at all.

This is the key to the distinction between fact and value. Values are selected from the range of possible future facts—or, for that matter, impossible ones—by an act of choice; they are not discovered in the world, but they are made and projected into the world. The term "project" is used by Sartre to distinguish the mode of being which men have from the mode of being which physical objects have: men *are* nothing more than physical objects, but they *undertake to be* something more. One of the most fundamental ways of achieving this human mode of being is negation, and Sartre's analysis of this is instructive for the present purpose.[2] If I enter a restaurant looking for my friend, the restaurant is as it is, with its tables, cus-

---

[1] Søren Kierkegaard, *Fear and Trembling* (with *The Sickness unto Death*), tr. W. Lowrie (New York: Doubleday Anchor Books, 1954), pp. 38–64, *passim.*

[2] Jean-Paul Sartre, *Being and Nothingness*, tr. H. Barnes (New York: Philosophical Library, 1956), pp. 9–10.

tomers, waiters, wine bottles, and so forth. But all this *being* is of no interest to me if my friend is not here; all this affirmation, from my point of view, can be summed up as a simple negation: he is not here. If I am anxious to find him, I must exchange this world for another in which he is more likely to be found, since that is the world to which I attach value. Objectively speaking, there are no negative facts, and no values; the world can be fully described, as it is, without resorting to either. But what this analysis overlooks is the fact that my world is incomplete without me; indeed it would not exist without me, and if I choose to inject into it negations and values, then no argument to the effect that these are unnecessary to a full description can prevent me from doing so. That is why every reductive account of the world, which denies freedom, or subjectivity, or value, is simply irrelevant. Everything such an account asserts about the world may be true, but what is true of *the* world is not necessarily true of *my* world. *My* world is the product of the temporal involvement of my subjectivity with *the* world, and it is to my world that values belong.

There is nothing inconsistent in adding that values very often belong in my world as phenomenologically *given;* the fact that something matters, while not evident to a detached observer—who will be satisfied that the objective account is exhaustive—stands as an indubitable datum to the subject whose involvement in the situation makes it matter. Values are not given, of course, as facts are given, by the agency of sense perception; the concept of *data* has to be enlarged to take account not only of the restrospective aspect of the world presently apprehended as fact, but also of its prospective aspect presently apprehended as value.

This leaves, it is true, an unresolved ambiguity between value as datum and value as project, between the given and the chosen. But it is precisely this ambiguity which makes possible the emergence of rational long-range projects. The first true experience of value may lie in a fear of some imminent pain, or of the imminent removal of some immediate pleasure, as directly given. Once it is understood, however, that the feared outcome does not *necessarily* ensue, a sense of *possibility* begins to develop, and this enables the agent to see beyond the overriding probabilities which are *given* as values (either positive or negative) to less likely alternatives which may be *chosen* as values and, with a little effort, also attained. A value once chosen and habitually pursued will gradually assume the character of the given, but it will remain a matter of habit (of "second nature") nevertheless. The same thing happens with facts: we become habituated to certain configurations, ensembles, sequences, and so forth which then appear given as wholes even when what is actually perceived is only a fragment of the whole. And there is nothing wrong with the process in either case—on the contrary it is a necessary simplification of the complexity of experience—provided that we are aware that it takes place.

VI
Freedom

THE PERVASIVENESS OF THE QUESTION OF FREEDOM. If values are future facts to which human subjects attach imperatives, it is clearly a matter of considerable interest whether or not these facts come about. Science can tell us, within limits, what future facts are probable (assuming no unexpected interference with the course of events), and it would, therefore, be possible to inquire what was most likely to happen and resolve to attach an imperative to that. The best way of being sure of getting what one wants is to want what one is probably going to get. And this would be the only rational thing to do if the course of future events were already determined, that is, if, given total knowledge, unexpected interference with it were to prove inconsistent with firmly established scientific discoveries. The Stoics believed that an immanent reason controlled the fate of the world and of mankind along with it, so that human actions were powerless to effect real change; they therefore recommended the willing acceptance of the inevitable as the only means of achieving internal harmony. Hegel, in a not wholly dissimilar argument, arrived at the conclusion that true freedom consisted in the voluntary acceptance of necessity. But the great majority of men have believed that what they as conscious subjects freely decided to do had a genuine effect on the future state of affairs, and they have therefore felt justified in ignoring considerations of probability and trying to bring about events which were not probable at all but only possible, and sometimes hardly that.

The admission that there is such a thing as conscious subjectivity—an admission that is difficult for a conscious subject not to make—raises all the old questions of the relation between that subjectivity and the world which it experiences. Such questions have absorbed the greater part of the attention of philosophers at all times, and the present is no exception; the philosophy of mind, and the so-called mind-body problem, are at the center of contemporary interest in the English-speaking world. Whatever solution may be proposed to this problem—identity or dualism, two-way interaction or epiphenomenalism—it is clear that the point of departure for an examination of it *must* lie in the subjectivity of the individual. Whatever he may have come to know or to assert about the mechanisms of perception or of action must be posterior to the "primordial dator consciousness" of perceiving and of acting, to use an expression of Husserl's. Arguments purporting to show that perception is really a complex chain of physiological causation which may lead to action without any involvement of consciousness forget that the apprehension and setting forth of the argument itself require such an involvement. It is true that a scientific account of action does not require any reference to subjectivity. From a vantage point outside the events dealt with, the argument for determinism can be carried through consistently, while the argument for freedom is clumsy and inconclusive. But of course the agent himself is not outside the events: he is a participant in them. From that internal perspective the maxim holds good that *even if men are not free, they cannot help behaving as if they were.*

Once the question takes on this *ad hominem* aspect—and it would be odd, in discussing human freedom, to leave it out—the two sides are better balanced. For in spite of differences in philosophical conviction men have certain overriding similarities of behavior, among them a common tendency to try to do something about it if things go wrong. The spectacle of a hard-boiled determinist struggling to change the world may of course be dismissed, by the determinist himself, as just another episode in the necessary unfolding of events. This argument might be correct, although there are good reasons—as will appear—for supposing that it is not. What is certain is that it cannot be refuted. But there is no reason why it should not simply be denied; the situation in which the burden of proof is considered to lie on the upholder of the efficacy of free action can be reversed by insisting that it really belongs, according to all criteria of plausibility and common sense, on the determinist side. The proponents of freedom have allowed themselves to be maneuvered into a defensive position, but they should really never have let this happen. The efficacy of volition is no queerer than the fact of perception.

NO DEMONSTRATION IS POSSIBLE. The mere denial of determinism is not, however, adequate as a guarantee of genuine freedom. It is a necessary but not a sufficient condition. The world might be totally chaotic, or partly determinate and partly probabilistic, and man be as helpless in the face of it as he would be if it were wholly determinate. To provide the sufficient condition we would have to show with scientific rigor that human agents—conscious subjects, where "subject" is understood in its phenomenological rather than its grammatical sense—can make a genuine difference to the course of events. But the character of scientific investigation works against the possibility of such a demonstration. Science is devoted to the establishment of invariable or statistically probable causal connections between states of affairs, and where human action is concerned it systematically bypasses the agent, as indeed for its own purposes it must. If a state of affairs a obtains at a given time t_1, then there is a probability $p(b/a)$ that a state of affairs b will obtain at a later time t_2. The times t_1 and t_2 are in a sense arbitrary; if time is continuous then any stretch of it, however short, which is defined by an initial t_1 and a terminal t_2, contains in principle infinitely many t_i (such that $t_1 < t_i < t_2$) which must be passed over in establishing causal connections between a and b. It is therefore always possible, in a case involving human action, to choose an a *before* the action takes place and a b *after* it takes place, and to establish a statistical connection between them (provided that a sufficient number of examples is available). According to the position advocated here, the agent occupies an inaccessible region of subjectivity into which the causal processes of perception disappear and from which the causal processes of action emerge; science jumps the gap and preserves the causal continuity, as Figure 3 shows. *a* and *b* may be pushed closer and closer together by refined techniques of psychological investigation—they certainly do not have to be outside the subject in a *physical* sense—without affecting the analysis. They can never be brought into coincidence; that would destroy the notion of causal *relatedness* altogether. But this applies in other cases as well. The fact that *a* and *b* are always separated by a finite interval of time means that *every* causal connection must jump over a discontinuity of this sort, and not only connec-

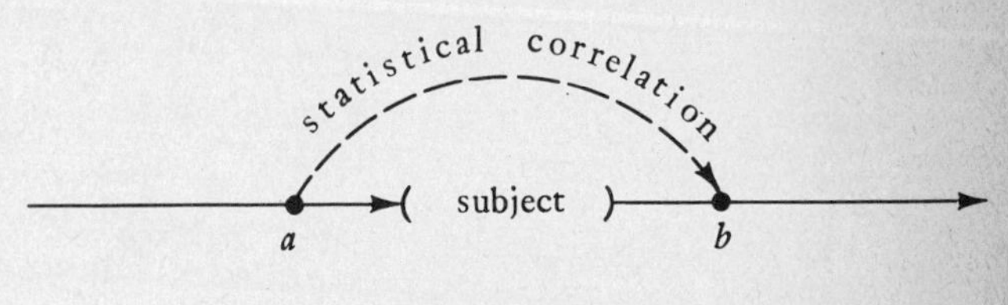

FIGURE 3

tions between the antecedents and consequences of human action—in fact every causal connection must jump over infinitely many of them.

This conclusion is implicit in the work of Hume. We see, he said, what we call causes and what we call effects, but no matter how finely we penetrate into the intermediate region we discover only other events of the same kind which are effects of the original causes or causes of the original effects; the connections themselves can never be discovered, but are always read into the situation by us *ex post facto*. There is a genuine connection in thought (a psychological connection) between the *idea* of the cause and the *idea* of the effect, but the assumption that this reflects an objective connection is unjustified. Of course it is not unreasonable to suppose that such a connection exists, since the world presumably hangs together somehow independently of its being *thought* together (although the idealist would maintain that its being thought together is precisely the mechanism of its hanging together); what is unreasonable is the simple-minded conclusion that the objective connection must be somehow *like* the connection in thought—for example, that if the latter is invariable the former must be so too, and so on. And yet the validity of this parallel between the causal and the logical is one of the fundamental assumptions of science, as was pointed out in Chapter IV. In science there is no reason to doubt the parallel—on the contrary it is extremely useful. (It remains an assumption nevertheless.) In the analysis of free action, on the other hand, there is every reason to doubt it; but people persist in carrying it over from science and using it to demonstrate that free action is impossible.

Even in science, as a matter of fact, invariable connections are the exception; and by a simple extension of a familiar analysis of probability, the possibility of free action can be reintroduced without abandoning the causal-logical parallel. It was remarked above that the fundamental scientific relation between an event a and an event b is expressed by the probability $p(b/a)$; if we adopt a subjective view of probability this represents an *expectation* that b will follow upon a. Now one of the marks of freedom on the part of the agent may reasonably be taken to be his ability to do something wholly unexpected—not unexpected by him, but unexpected by an outside observer equipped with a complete history of his previous behavior. A wholly unexpected event would of course have a probability of zero, and it is ordinarily assumed that a probability of zero on the logical side corresponds to physical impossibility on the causal side. But it can be shown[1] that this interpretation rests on a misunderstanding of the axioms of probability, and that there is nothing inconsistent in the notion that an event with a logical probability of zero might nevertheless happen. This is certainly provided for in ordinary language ("I would *never* have expected him to do that"), and it reflects our intuitive conviction that action can genuinely be the beginning of a finite causal chain and not simply an element somewhere along an infinite one.

The question of the agent's ability to do the unexpected brings into focus what I take to be the central difficulty in the philosophical dispute about freedom and determinism. A good deal of work has recently been devoted to showing that the dispute is unnecessary—that there is no inconsistency between the language of freedom in moral discourse and the language of determinism in scientific discourse, that the problems of philosophical ethics would not be affected one way or the other by a decision about determinism, that free (uncoerced) actions make sense in a physically determined world while free (uncaused) actions do not make sense at all, and so forth. In particular the important thesis of D. M. McKay,[2] which offers a means of reconciling an agent's insistence that the outcome of his actions cannot be known with an observer's insistence that it can, has moved the

[1] Peter Caws, "Three Logics, or the Possibility of the Improbable," *Philosophy and Phenomenological Research*, XXV, 4 (June 1965), 615–26.

[2] D. M. McKay, "Information and Prediction in Human Sciences," in S. Dockx and P. Bernays, eds., *Information and Prediction in Science* (New York and London: Academic Press, 1965), p. 255.

debate to a new level of rigor, although I do not think it has solved the problem. For a cardinal difficulty remains, which has to do not with the possibility of a reconciliation of freedom and determinism in objective terms—that is, for human agents in general, or for some anonymous agent—but with *my own* involvement in *my own* action. If I say of an action: "I did it," or "I was in full control of myself when I did it," as a way of accepting responsibility or claiming credit, I cannot at the same time say that the action was uncaused; but nor can I admit that it was wholly caused by some antecedent set of circumstances, and could in principle have been expected by a sufficiently well-informed observer, as any determinist account would require. For this would involve the paradoxical assertion that events which were *not* under my control (and such events would certainly be arrived at if the causal chain were pushed back far enough) had fully determined an action which *was* under my control.

SOME PRE-ANALYTIC CONSIDERATIONS. The alternatives offered above (actions as uncaused, actions as wholly caused by physical antecedents) cannot be considered exhaustive if there is to be any escape from this difficulty. The route of escape lies, however, in another dimension, out of the plane of phenomenal causality altogether, as Kant rightly saw. It can therefore be taken only existentially, never discursively, and we all do take it, as a matter of course, every time we say "*I* did it." Determinism can never establish itself in the face of that assertion, for its establishment would require the demonstration of tight causal relations, every step in which would have to be physically self-contained, between the antecedents and consequences of action; and the conscious subject, which is not physical at all (it is conscious *of* the physical) persists in intruding itself between these antecedents and consequences and spoiling the whole program. It is not so much that the conscious subject is *un*determined, *non*-material, *un*intelligible, as that it is *prior* to the concepts of determination, materiality, and intelligibility.

It is enough for our purpose to be satisfied that the issue is not settled in favor of determinism, and the foregoing remarks may be sufficient for this end. That much has to be insisted upon because many people feel uncomfortable about their own control over their own actions in a world which they believe to have been shown, at least in principle, to be determined with respect to gross phenomena, among which human actions must certainly be counted. This negative way is not, however, the only one that is open to us. There are some arguments of a non-philosophical kind which provide further reasons for asserting the possibility of non-phenomenal causality, and which may be worth a moment's attention. Clearly there are living organisms whose actions are straightforward responses to the stimuli which impinge upon them, the connection between stimulus and response being linear and determinate. As far as that is concerned, many actions performed by human agents appear to fall into this class: blinking, knee jerks, and so on, as well as more complicated learned responses. But such reflex or habitual actions, the causal mechanism of which does not involve consciousness or decision, do not count as *actions* at all in the sense in which the term will be used here (etymologically speaking, its use to refer to the behavior of inanimate objects or to involuntary bodily mechanisms is secondary). The evolutionary origins of genuine action lie in the development of a cortical brain from a diencephalic one. The diencephalon, or brain stem, channels neural energy directly from stimulus to response; the cortex, on the other hand, diverts the energy from the stimulus and temporarily absorbs it, feeding it into the mechanism of response after a period of delay which represents the activity of choice, or sometimes suppressing the response altogether. Conscious deliberation, leading to the delayed and selective action which we call voluntary, appears to be associated with the advanced development of the cortex, found among terrestrial animals only in man and some of the higher mammals. The interesting question, from the point of view of evolution, is: why should the animal be *conscious?* If we reject the view, held by Descartes among others, that consciousness is a superaddition in the case of man which distinguishes him absolutely from the animals, we must assign to it an effective role in the preservation of the species and assume that it makes a genuine difference to the outcome of action. Any theory, from which it follows that the history of the conscious animal is just what it would have been if it had happened not to be conscious, makes consciousness a mystery and opens the way to all kinds of metaphysical nonsense. Of course the admission that consciousness has an evolutionary origin and significance does not mean the advocacy of a so-called "evolutionary ethics," such as that developed by Spencer, for example, or by Nietzsche. The evolutionary argument points to the efficacy of conscious volition but does not indicate the ends which that volition should seek.

It must be admitted that the *nature* of the free subject remains obscure, but perhaps this is just as well. There is, after all, something inconsistent in the notion of the subject's understanding himself completely, and it is easy to see that it leads to an infinite regress: if I understand myself, am I identical with that which I understand, or is there a separate movement in which I understand myself-as-understood? Consciousness of the world, as Sartre points out, is at the same time consciousness of one's own being as a knower, and one might add that action in the world is at the same time consciousness of one's own being as an agent—the "pre-reflective *cogito*" [3] is matched by a "pre-reflective *ago*," the "I" in each case being implicit in the knowing or the acting. But *understanding* or *explaining* one's own being or one's own action is a different matter, and cannot have this pre-reflective unity, since it requires three terms: the thing explained, the explanation, and the person to whom the explanation explains the thing. One of the consequences of this analysis is that there must be three ultimately inexplicable concepts, namely the self, the world as a whole, and the relation between the two (that is, the apprehension by the self of the world as a whole, together with its inverse, the action of the self on the world as a whole). An adequate analysis of free agency would involve the explication of these inexplicable concepts, and this means that it is not merely a difficult but a logically impossible task. Kant's noumenal self, and Sartre's nothingness—the two most impressive attempts at a resolution of this problem of the free agent—therefore miss the point; and it goes without saying that no substitute for them will be offered here.

FREE AGENCY RETAINED AS AN UNREFUTED HYPOTHESIS. If rational justification of man's freedom is futile, practical demonstration is equally so. Freedom has no function unless it enables men to achieve what they

[3] Jean-Paul Sartre, *Being and Nothingness*, tr. H. Barnes (New York: Philosophical Library, 1956), p. liii.

set out to achieve, but the antecedent intention to achieve it can always be pointed to as determining the action in question, which is then said after all not to have been free. This difficulty cannot be side-stepped by a so-called "gratuitous act," since that would not count as free either, its effect not having been seriously intended at all and certainly not desired. In order to *show* that he was free, a man would have to do something he wished, and at the same time did not wish, to do.

But I repeat again that all these contortions are unnecessary. Our conscious subjectivity confronts the world: within the limits of our apprehension we seek to understand the world—that is, to relate its various parts correctly—and within the limits of our freedom we seek to change the world—that is, to realize its possibilities correctly. At these limits, as Kant points out in his characteristic manner, the intellect is forced to admit its own inadequacy:

> Two things fill the mind with ever new and increasing admiration and awe, the oftener and more steadily they are reflected on: the starry heavens above me and the moral law within me.[4]

But both dimensions are given in experience; and whatever difficulties their reconciliation may present, no solution which eliminates one altogether can, in the long run, be acceptable.

The admission of limitations on the intellect need not, of course, be construed as a hint that something greater lies *beyond* the intellect. It is often supposed that the rationality of man argues a Rationality of the Universe, as though the fact (which we know to be

---

[4] Immanuel Kant, *Critique of Practical Reason*, tr. L. W. Beck (Univ. of Chicago Press, 1949), p. 258.

true) that rationality is the product of an extremely complicated physical organization were evidence that this extremely complicated physical organization is a product of rationality. This is obviously silly, but on some such argument rests one of the most persuasive cases against freedom. It is a variation on the Stoic position, and maintains that rational action may be free vis-à-vis the physical world and yet determined in a larger setting as the working out of a purpose higher than ourselves. If this is a conscious purpose the problem simply emerges on a higher level, since the limitations referred to are logically inherent in the very notion of subjectivity and must inevitably attach themselves to any consciousness whatever; and, in any case, for the individual, the situation is no improvement over purely physical determination and cannot subjectively be distinguished from it.

Perhaps the most fundamental objection to the efficacy of free action springs from the dualism of mind and body which it seems to require. In the quotation from Kant given above, the inner being to which the moral law appeals is of a different order from the outer being of the starry heavens, and yet the realm of freedom to which the former belongs must somehow interact with the realm of nature symbolized by the latter. (In Kant the inner form of intuition is time, and the location of the moral law within provides an incidental reinforcement of the connection between time and value.) None of the monistic devices for the reconciliation of freedom with determinism has disposed convincingly of the fact that I am not the world on which I exert my action and that my freedom is merely illusory if it cannot introduce genuine novelty into that world. This point has to be faced honestly. As I have said, I offer no solution to the difficulty, but I have tried to indicate some respects in which the implicit reductivism of the contemporary philosophy of mind encounters difficulties of its own. It is only an insistence on a causally tight universe (and therefore a monistic one, if category confusions are to be avoided) which makes the problem of free action so vexing and places such an unbridgeable chasm between the subject and his world. A shift in the burden of proof, so that it is the causal tightness rather than freedom which requires to be demonstrated, will provide ample leisure for exploring the consequences of the hypothesis of efficacious subjective volition.

VII
Order

ORDER AS RELATIVE TO HUMAN INTEREST. The rational exercise of my freedom consists in changing my world (or protecting it against change) in such a way as to realize my values. The world can be counted on to change, of course, even if I do nothing; it obeys its own laws of development and decay. My intervention is called for if it appears that a future state of the world, to which I attach an imperative, will not come about naturally, or if it appears that a present state to whose maintenance I attach an imperative is in danger of dissolution. And this means constant intervention, since every situation, left to itself, changes by slow degrees into something else, and in any case few situations which occur naturally are likely to be those I want. Any particular state of the world is antecedently improbable, since the natural course of things on a macroscopic scale is determined, as far as we can tell, wholly at random; the chances that the state which happens to be realized at a given moment in the history of the universe will meet the very exigent specifications of individual human desire are therefore infinitesimally small.

This fact, which is obvious after a moment's reflection, is generally concealed from us by two circumstances. First, the evolution of animal species, of which man is one, takes place in such a way that any population which survives at all finds itself in an environment to which it is reasonably well adapted. The probability that physical conditions suitable to life as we know it should be realized in any particular region of space and time is very low, and if the life had been created independently, and had then sought the conditions, the conjunction of the two would be nothing short of miraculous. But in fact the conditions determined the nature of the life. Cosmically speaking, the biosphere is a vanishingly thin shell on a microscopic particle, but it required no intelligence on our part to locate it and make our home in it. Second, although nature—even when the animal species is well adapted to it—is on the whole hostile to the individual, herd living and its subsequent development into civilization have provided a collective defense against this hostility, so that nowadays most individual men have to expend very little effort on securing and maintaining conditions of reasonable comfort. (That subsistence is now relatively easy is in itself one of the determinants of the crisis of value. An animal equipped by a long history of necessity to make frequent adjustments in its environment tends to go on making adjustments even when the necessity is removed; if no change is obviously called for, the alternatives are invention or frustration. Food and shelter are the obvious values of men who are hungry and cold, but the values of men who are satisfied and comfortable are not quite so easily discovered.)

What civilization helps to guarantee is a degree of *order*—domestic, social, civil, and international. Order in these senses is something to be striven for and something which, once achieved, must be actively maintained. It therefore has precisely the character of value, and in fact the realization of a value is always equivalent to the achievement and maintenance of an order, not necessarily of the public variety referred to above, but in one way or another the disposition of the elements of a situation in a satisfactory or acceptable way. While the term "order" seems originally to have applied to things organized in rows—for example, citizens in order of rank or precedence—it soon came to mean any proper arrangement, social or otherwise, extending eventually even to the order of nature.

Nature seems ordered to us, of course, because of the fact that we are adapted to its regularities. But it is important to realize that the expression "the order of nature," taken as descriptive of the physical universe, is vacuous. No matter what may be the case, no matter how chaotic or disorganized the behavior of the elements of the world, still at every moment each thing is where it is, standing in a definite and, in principle, describable relation to each other thing. Such a situation can be thought of as disorder only by contrast to other situations which, under the circumstances, might be expected or preferred, and the notions of expectation or preference introduce the by now familiar syndrome of temporality and value. The dying man in Eliot's "Animula,"

Leaving disordered papers in a dusty room;

regrets his failure to achieve a certain kind of value, but in a sense the room is fully ordered, every paper and every particle of dust occupying its fixed and proper place. The word "proper" is appropriate only if we have an interest in preserving that particular room in that particular state—a perfectly plausible objective for an artist working with assemblages, for example, or for a collector of literary relics if it happened to be Eliot's own room. Here the conventional notions of order and disorder are reversed, and the unsuspecting maid who came in and dusted, put the papers in neat piles, and so on, would be accused of having destroyed something of irreplaceable value.

These considerations point to a definition of order in such everyday contexts: we shall say that a state of affairs is ordered in some way if a change in it matters, and that it is maximally ordered if any change would be a change for the worse. In a library in which everything is out of order, it does not matter if the positions of two books on a shelf are interchanged, but if the books are in alphabetical order it does matter. Again, if the books are out of order but it matters that they should be in order—if their being in order is a state of the world it is desired to achieve—a process of ordering can be carried out, starting from a situation of relative chaos in which arbitrary changes make no difference and ending with a fully ordered situation in which an arbitrary change would be destructive. Libraries are a special case; more generally I repeat that any action which seeks to realize a value amounts to the imposition of some order on the world or to the safeguarding of an existing order against the threat of disorder.

THE THERMODYNAMIC CONCEPT OF ORDER. The achievement of order requires the expenditure of energy, and it can therefore be attempted only when energy is available. Even the maintenance of order requires available energy; the natural tendency of ordered situations is to become disordered if care is not taken to preserve them—as ruins, neglected gardens, untidy apartments, littered streets, and wrinkled clothes all testify. Human energy spends itself in a series of orderings against a series of natural tendencies to disorder, and the series manifests itself on every scale of existence, from the daily routine of personal habit to the rise and fall of civilizations. The improbability of the emergence of useful order without the expenditure of energy is expressed in the second law of thermodynamics. Strictly speaking, the laws of thermodynamics apply only to expenditures and transfers of energy in the form of heat, but some of the concepts involved have proved irresistibly suggestive to workers in other disciplines and have acquired a much more general currency. Chief among these is the concept of entropy.

Entropy, roughly speaking, is a measure of disorder, a measure of the randomness of the distribution of energy in a physical system. A closed system—that is, one which receives no energy from outside—will, if left to itself, gradually lose whatever order it had. If its elements are very carefully organized at the beginning, so that their energy is not distributed at random at all but coherently directed, the entropy of the system is at a minimum; but as time goes on the elements will gradually lose their definite relationships to one another, the coherence of energy will disappear, and the entropy will eventually rise to a maximum.

This will happen most rapidly if the organized energy is made available for the performance of external work. In an automobile engine the explosion touched off by the spark organizes the energy of the reacting particles very briefly, by causing them to move rapidly away from one another; those which happen to be moving in the direction of the piston therefore perform work upon it, while the others waste their energy on the walls of the cylinder. When this brief episode is over and the piston has moved, the particles continue to move about in the cylinder with very great speed, but now they move at random, some in one direction and some in another, some towards other particles, some away from them. They are therefore good for nothing but to be swept out as exhaust and replaced by another population of temporarily organized particles. The temporary organization is conferred upon the new set of particles, as upon the old set, by the chemical energy released in the process of ignition. During the chemical reaction which releases this energy the system of particles is not closed, but open, at least as far as its mechanical energy is concerned; it is only after the chemical process is over that it functions briefly as a closed system, subject to the second law of thermodynamics and therefore to a rapid increase in entropy and a rapid decrease in useful order.

It must be remarked that the second law does not say that order in a system can *never* increase—it says this only of closed systems. Whenever, therefore, there is a noticeable concentration of order in the natural world, we may reasonably expect to find an open system, one which enjoys a supply of energy from some external source. The biosphere, in which animals (including man) have evolved, civilizations grown up, and works of art been produced, is such a system; it receives daily from the sun very large quantities of energy in the form of radiation. The presence of matter anywhere in the universe represents a concentration of enormous amounts of energy—an idea that is becoming familiar in an age of nuclear weapons and atomic submarines—and the sun represents the concentration of an enormous amount of matter, at least according to our standards (as stars go, it is rather small). This matter is continually being augmented as the sun's gravitational attraction sweeps up a great tubular region of interstellar dust in its progress through space, but it is also continually being attenuated by radiation, and the reserves are growing steadily less. This radiation, of which the earth collects only a minute fraction (since radiation leaves the sun in all directions whereas the earth is to be found only in one direction at any given time), has been going on for a very long time and will continue for an even longer time in the future. The time scale dwarfs anything that we can have any real conception of, but it is well to remember that the situation of cosmic privilege which we now enjoy was not always the case and will not always be so. In the last few million years, which are the only ones that really count for our purposes, the earth has stored a great deal of the energy it has received from the sun in chemical and biological traps which we know as mineral deposits,[1] vegetation, and animal life. As might be expected, this trapped energy shows up not merely as matter in motion, but as *ordered* matter, the order being an inevitable consequence of the constant influx of new energy. And the

[1] Deposits of the heavy elements (e.g., metals) come, however, from a different process at an earlier stage of the earth's formation.

concentration of higher levels of order in cities, libraries, and museums reflects again the availability of surplus energy in its intermediate forms—food, fuel, hydroelectic power, and so on. Virtually all this available energy can be traced back to the sun, although we are now beginning to learn to be independent of the sun by turning the material of the earth itself into energy.

HUMAN AGENTS AS SOURCES OF ORDER. The definition of order in terms of what matters has been quite forgotten in all this discussion of thermodynamics, or so it would appear. But in fact the thermodynamic concept of order is shot through with implicit references to value. "Available energy" and "useful work" are too obvious to require comment, but even the classical formulations of the second law of thermodynamics reveal a preoccupation with the achievement of particular ends. The second law states that it is impossible to devise an engine to effect the transfer of heat from a cooler body to a warmer one unless it is provided with an external source of energy. This statement has been referred to by the scientists themselves as "a confession of our helplessness in making molecules do what we wish" [2]; the law is formulated in terms of impossibility only because what it excludes was once thought possible. Although its rigorous formulation is due to Clausius the principle which underlies it was discovered by the French physicist Carnot in the course of his work on heat engines, and represented an unexpected theoretical limitation on the efficiency of such engines. If the law were not true, an unlimited source of mechanical energy would be at our disposal,

---

[2] "Thermodynamics," *Van Nostrand's Scientific Encyclopedia*, 3rd ed. (Princeton: Van Nostrand, 1958).

and early physicists were disappointed to discover that this was not the case. The impossibility is a human impossibility which deprives us of something we would have liked to have. The law of gravity might have been formulated in terms of impossibility: it is impossible to devise an engine (ruling out balloons and other floating devices) which will go upwards unless it is provided with an external source of energy (which may be stored "inside" the engine as chemical energy for convenience in transportation). The law of gravity was not formulated in this way, however, because until recently nobody had very much interest in going upwards.

The state of the world we want, then, is for us order; and the antecedent possibility of getting it by accident is negligibly small. And yet many of us do get it, or something close to it, and not only in the plain evolutionary sense that we are well adapted to our environment and enjoy the benefits of civilization, but much more specifically: we form the intention of changing the environment in a specific way, and actually bring about such a change; we paint paintings, compose musical works, write books, play games, build and furnish houses, travel (that is, change the environment by bringing new parts of it into view), undertake commercial enterprises, and so on. Drawing the line between what we owe to the impersonal processes of evolution and the personal processes of decision is not always easy, and a plausible argument could be made for regarding the latter simply as an individual version of the former, or, conversely, the former as a collective version of the latter. But each of us can recognize that there are some orders (for example, the daily, monthly, and yearly rhythms of terrestrial life) which we owe to nature, and others (for example, the disposition of our private belongings and the arrangement of books on shelves) which we owe to our own efforts or to the efforts of people like us. Which class properly includes large-scale human phenomena like cities and armies is a question for debate, but at all events it is clear that the lines of causal determination of all but the grossest forms of order in our environment pass through human individuals, and that such individuals constitute a locus for the reversal of the cosmic tendency towards disorder. Human agents, in fact, are sources of negative entropy; and when all is said and done, it is that which makes them free. Even under such local violations the second law of thermodynamics continues to assert itself, since the brain of each human provides him at birth with a far greater degree of organization than he is ever likely to impose unaided on the world about him. But the question is a relative one; he needs only enough surplus organizing power to fight more or less successfully, for seventy years or so, a battle against disorder which in the end he will inevitably lose.

All order matters. What we sometimes call the order of nature—the relative densities of different substances, the alternation of night and day, the balance of hormones—consists just in those arrangements which if changed would affect our interests most profoundly. When in fact there are serious lapses in this order we call them disasters. Most aspects of natural order are such that we can do very little about them except on a limited and local scale; human order, on the other hand, is something we are continually in the process of creating. There is no limit to the degree of human order that can be conceived. But material resources are limited, and the freedom of the individual, while within the limits of its material resources it is in principle unfettered, is in fact to a considerable degree preoccupied with the maintenance of often idiosyncratic conditions for the possibility of any action at all. (This explains why so many people in such apparently privileged circumstances achieve so little of lasting value.) Maintaining the conditions for action—keeping oneself, as it were, continually poised to achieve value, even if one never actually achieves it—is clearly the next best thing to acting, and even better than acting unwisely. It embodies in itself a kind of value. To use our earlier terminology, a state of the world so arranged, that from it one could move in the most economical way possible to *any* desired state of the world, is itself a desirable state. The value attaching to it is of the kind that has traditionally been called *instrumental*, as distinguished from the *terminal* value of the state of the world which is the ultimate objective.

The practical problems of the theory of value, moral, political, and aesthetic, lie in deciding which states of the world deserve to have terminal values attached to them, which states instrumental values, and how the limited material resources and the limited freedom of human agents can best be deployed to bring these states about. To put it differently, the fundamental problem is to find out what matters to the agent, how it can be reconciled with other things that matter to him, or that matter to other agents, and how the fact of its mattering can be accommodated in action.

THE CAPACITY FOR ORDER AN UNCONDITIONAL VALUE. If there were an independent criterion of order, and if every order embodied a value—if, that is to say, order mattered only positively—there would be an easy solution to the problems of the theory of value. The overriding moral principle would be: seek to achieve order; and the theory of value would become a branch of thermodynamics. This idea has in fact been developed by a contemporary physicist, R. B. Lindsay,[3] who has introduced the idea of a "thermodynamic imperative." But unfortunately, while every value can be represented as an order, every order cannot be represented as a value. Maximally ordered systems, according to the definition given above, do represent, it is true, extremes of value along some dimension or other. But that might be just making the best of a bad job, and the desired state of the world might lie along some other dimension altogether. Any change *in the actual situation* would be a change for the worse, but we still might want to exchange that situation for a totally different one. In such a case it would be necessary to retreat to a point at which the shift into another dimension of value could be accomplished, a strategy that is familar from the cliché about things getting worse before they get better.

The idea of a generalized imperative based on a thermodynamic argument need not be abandoned, however, just because what thermodynamics recognizes as order is not necessarily what we value. The surplus energy of the environment is bound to show up as order, and for us the important thing is that we are able to have a part in determining to some extent what the nature of that order shall be. If the source of this personally determined order is the freedom of the agent to manipulate the world, to which he has access through his body, then a genuine moral principle (or at least a general principle of value) emerges, namely that this freedom, and the body which exer-

[3] R. B. Lindsay, "Entropy Consumption and Values in Physical Science," *American Scientist*, XLVII (September 1959), 376–85.

cises it, should be safeguarded. The state of the world in which freedom and bodily efficiency are optimized must have an imperative attached to it if any subsequent state of the world is marked as a value. In other words, failure to value freedom is incompatible with the realization of any other value. The question at issue here is not whether one man's freedom is better than another's, but whether freedom in the most general sense—that is, the ability not necessarily to suspend the causal order but at least to halt or reverse temporarily and locally the universal trend towards disorder—is to be regarded as an unconditional imperative for any conscious production of value. The argument of this chapter has been devoted to showing that this is an inevitable conclusion.

It is clear, of course, that human consciousness is not the only source of local negative entropy. The other sources, however, have either disappeared or settled down into an ecologically stable relationship to one another. Man is the only animal engaged in the systematic and continuous production of new order. At the same time it is in man that the largest fund of conscious awareness, at least in the world known to him, appears to be vested. Consciousness itself, Schrödinger thought,[4] may simply be a concomitant of the emergence of novelty: when a man is learning to ride a bicycle, he is conscious of the adjustments in his position, and so forth, which are necessary to prevent him from falling off; once he has learned to ride, however, these adjustments become habitual and he is no longer consciously aware of them. The implications of this view are far-reaching and will not be

---

[4] Erwin Schrödinger, *Mind and Matter* (Cambridge Univ. Press, 1959), pp. 4–5.

pursued here, but it does suggest an important difference between free action and other forms of adaptive behavior. If the order sought is a standard one, for a species or for an individual, then its achievement can be programmed. The process, like all adaptive processes, will involve feedback, but the nature of the feedback will *determine* the nature of the adaptive response, which can therefore be automatic or habitual. If, on the other hand, the required order is not a function of the present state of affairs but is open—if in fact it is not yet *required* in Köhler's sense[5]—then the conscious entertainment of alternatives is probably a good deal more efficient, from an evolutionary point of view, in achieving it than is the incorporation of a random factor into the program, which would otherwise be necessary. If there are very few alternatives and if, as we say, there is not much to choose between them, randomizing is an acceptable solution. Of course a program can be written—for example, for playing chess—to take into account alternatives following upon alternatives to any desired degree of complexity, but it has to terminate in the definite acceptance or rejection of the strategy being tested, and this requires a prior decision about the object of the game.

Reason is, in a way, a completely general program for the resolution of choice, but it needs to be supplied with a conception of the order that is to result, and it seems to be the function of consciousness to contribute this. The order chosen, if the choice is free and rational, will by definition be one which embodies a value. It is certainly true for the individual, and it may, if Schrödinger's conjecture has any validity, be

[5] Wolfgang Köhler, *The Place of Value in a World of Facts* (New York: Liveright, 1938), Chap. III.

true for the species, that there is a progressive selection among values and a progressive development of habitual, as opposed to conscious, choice, the former being adequate once a decision about the desired order has been made and the mechanism for arriving at it put into operation.

VIII
Action and Responsibility

THE COMPLEXITY OF FREE ACTION. Every manifestation of order which goes beyond the merely physical or biological can be traced back to an *agent*, that is, to an individual who is a locus of freedom and whose exercise of this freedom, either by himself or in co-operation with others, modifies the subsequent state of the world—often predictably, but sometimes in a manner which is unpredictable on the basis of the most complete knowledge of its previous state. Freedom as understood here manifests itself *only* in agents, and for our purposes—even though there might be a certain looseness in the causal structure of the physical world elsewhere than in the human brain, of which other free agents might take advantage—we need consider human agency, and therefore human action, only.

If free action is to result in a change in the order of the world it must have access to the world, and this is effected by means of the body. The body stores and disposes of a certain amount of energy, sufficient by itself to produce minor changes but capable of amplification—by cooperation with others, or by means of more or less complex tools—so as to produce major ones. Freedom to produce a particular change (in other words, to realize a particular value) depends on the availability of the requisite energy, disposed in a suitable way, and this means that the agent must enjoy a degree of material privilege over the world he seeks to modify. The change brought about by the expenditure of this energy is a movement of the world from one state to another which is presumably preferable. In order for the agent to be in control of the situation it is therefore not enough for him to have command of the material resources; he must also have access in detail to information about the initial state, and he must know accurately how states of the world respond to given expenditures of energy, that is, he must know the scientific laws governing the case. The formulation of the laws need not be technically sophisticated—the conditions are met by somebody who knows that pottery is fragile, who has the energy of the gravitational field at his disposal, and who knows that objects released from rest fall. If he has a vase in his hand he is free to drop it, and it will break.

Two other conditions for free action must be added to make the specification complete, as this example makes clear: first, the man must wish to break the vase (if he dropped it by accident, we would not say he had performed an action at all), and second, nobody must prevent him from carrying out his intention. The idea of freedom turns out to be much more complex, when embodied in action, than it is in its metaphysically pure form. We cannot in fact claim that an action is free unless the agent:

(1) intends to achieve a given end by it,[1]
(2) is not restrained by another agent,
(3) has suitable resources of energy and material at his disposal,
(4) has sufficient information about the state of the world at the time of the action, and
(5) knows the laws governing the behavior of that world and hence the consequences of his action.

Most of the conditions in this list, taken by themselves, are perfectly obvious, but their conjunction is what I want to insist upon. If any one of the conditions is not met in connection with some action or set of actions, then the concept of freedom in that connection is empty. Slaves are not free, and most people are in agreement about that; what is not always so clear is that poor men are not free either, and even powerful men are not free if they are ignorant. There is of course a sense in which ignorant men are free to investigate their circumstances so as to remove their ignorance, and this is clearly the situation of the scientist. It would be absurd to insist that the laws an experiment was designed to establish should be known in advance as a condition for the freedom of the experimentation. But this does not invalidate the fifth condition, since the successful achievement of the scientific end does depend on a knowledge of the regularities of the physical world against which those of the experiment are to be measured.

MORALITY AN INTERPERSONAL CONCEPT. Nothing has

[1] Note that this does not imply that he actually achieves the end in question.

so far been said about morality. Before that subject could be approached it was necessary to establish, at least for the purposes of argument, that there are such things as free actions; for while it is not the case that all free actions are morally significant, it certainly is the case that all morally significant actions are free. A morally significant action I take to be one for which the agent can reasonably be praised or blamed, rewarded or punished. The definition works best with praise and blame, since reward and punishment can be understood in purely behavioristic terms as stimulating or inhibiting future actions of the same kind. Praise and blame, as far as that goes, *can* be viewed in the behavioristic way too, if they are communicated to the agent, but they are to be regarded here as objective judgments. From the point of view of the subject it would seem unfair to *be blamed* for something he could not help, for an action in other words which he was not free to avoid, and I am content for the time being to leave the matter on that level.

For reasons which will become clear in the next chapter (and must be implicitly obvious already), I shall restrict the adjective "moral" to actions affecting the freedom of other agents. This amounts to a rejection of the concept of a "desert-island" morality, but it still reflects accurately most of the ordinary meanings of the term which do not depend on transcendent presuppositions. The principal difficulty is with actions traditionally called *prudential* (such as giving up smoking because it is dangerous to health), some of which on this analysis fall outside the moral realm altogether. No action which is *wholly* reflexive, even if it enhances or impairs the freedom of the agent, is to be judged in moral terms. It is sometimes said that there never could be such an action, except perhaps on the desert island itself, but in fact there are large numbers of private actions whose probable consequences reach no further than the agent. It might perhaps be argued that a man who committed suicide or became an incurable alcoholic, even if these actions had no social effects (which is admittedly unlikely in such cases), would commit a moral offense against a potential future self whose freedom was affected by them; he might even take this view himself. But moral indignation directed at oneself on account of actions affecting nobody but oneself has a certain artificiality about it. Jekyll loathed Hyde, but that was because Hyde had murdered an innocent man. If an action of mine affects my future freedom—and many actions do—I may call myself stupid or clever, but I shall not, unless I have a very exalted idea of my own importance, consider myself to have done anything moral or immoral, or worthy of praise or blame. I *can* blame myself for a genuinely immoral action, such as failure to help a drowning man; in this case I identify myself with, and take the part of, the other members of a society to which he and I both belong. They would regard such a failure as immoral. But I cannot take their part against myself when no other person is involved, for according to this analysis they themselves ought to admit that my reflexive action carries no moral weight.

The fact that many people have believed that reflexive actions can be moral or immoral, so that persons committing them have felt commended or blamed by society, is just another example of the overloading of the concept of morality to which reference has already been made. What has generally been in the back of their minds, of course, is that there could not really be such a thing as a wholly reflexive action, since God sees and judges all. But this is a *non sequitur*. For unless God's freedom were impaired by his witnessing the action—which is absurd—it would, if wholly reflexive, be amoral by this criterion *even if God were looking*. Of course if morality is to be defined in terms of arbitrary standards laid down by God, the popular belief may be correct, but in this case "moral" ceases to have any useful meaning.

MORAL RESPONSIBILITY AND CAUSAL RESPONSIBILITY. It may help in setting the boundaries within which moral considerations properly apply if we attempt a rudimentary classification of voluntary actions. Such actions—that is, those performed by a free agent for a deliberate end—fall into four clearly distinguishable classes. These are not exhaustive, although they account for most cases, and they overlap, since actions are rarely simple. On the lowest level are what I call *sustaining* actions: actions which do not set out to increase or decrease the amount of order in the world but which concern the maintenance of the human organism, such as getting up in the morning, eating, taking exercise, working for a living, and so on. These actions would not take place unless they were voluntarily performed, but in themselves they serve no value beyond the simple survival of the individual or the species. Continuous with this class are *conventional* or *ritual* actions like putting on a tie, shaking hands, applauding a performance, and the like. Third come distinctly *moral* (or immoral) actions, freely undertaken because of their effect on the freedom of others, such as giving to charity or shooting one's enemies. And, finally, *aesthetic* actions comprise all those done for the sake of some quality in their results which changes the order of the world, without affecting the freedom of others, so that the world comes closer to the agent's conception of what it ought to be.

Few actions which are not simple fall neatly into any one of these classes; the point is to identify very roughly the major reasons for acting at all. Sustaining actions preserve the status quo on the individual level, ritual actions preserve it on the social level; moral actions preserve or change it for other people (sustaining actions performed by an individual on behalf of the community are automatically moral, unless they are performed only for pay), while aesthetic actions change it for the agent and perhaps also for other people. The chief departure from ordinary usage here concerns the meaning of "aesthetic," which is considerably widened. This is no accident—in fact it is of fundamental importance—and in a later chapter it will be dealt with in greater detail.

Sustaining, conventional, or aesthetic actions may of course *become* moral or immoral because it turns out that they have an effect on the freedom of others, even though this was not intended. But the line must be carefully drawn here, because it would be absurd to hold a man morally responsible for an improbable and wholly unforeseen consequence of an innocent act. Moralists have always been fond of edifying stories about missing nails and lost battles, great oaks and little acorns, and so forth, but while these have a legitimate point it is obviously not possible to spend all one's time in conjecture as to the possible outcome of minor actions. One ought, of course, to be aware of any *likely* outcome, and behave accordingly; and in the estimation of what counts as likely it is better to err on the side of caution and restraint than on the side of confidence and daring where the freedom of others is concerned. (In the case of consequences affecting only oneself, as we have seen, moral considerations do not apply.) But it is perfectly possible for a man to be the *causal* agent of some event without being its *moral* agent, even though the event is one which, if brought about deliberately, would lead us to condemn the agent as immoral.

Moral responsibility is thus a special case of causal responsibility. The term "responsible," by itself, is ambiguous, and one of the most serious tasks of ethics is to decide at what point the moral meaning becomes operative. Morally sensitive men will be concerned about the possible consequences of their actions, but to what lengths should such sensitivity go? At one end of the scale, the man who removed a sign saying "danger" at the edge of a cliff because it obstructed his view would generally be thought to have done something immoral; at the other, a man of no public importance, who refused a drink at a crowded bar on the grounds that his example might corrupt the young, would not be thought to have done anything particularly moral. But consider the case of Albert Szent-Györgyi, who, when awarded the Nobel Prize, insisted on investing the money in "shares which had to go down in the case of war," [2] because of his belief that war was wrong. Was that a quixotic gesture to be dismissed, or a moral example to be followed? There are clearly two parts to the question, one having to do with the consistency of the action with the belief, the other with the validity of the belief itself, but it is the former which concerns us here. The question is, not only what *are* the probable consequences of my action, but also how much I know (or want to know)

[2] Albert Szent-Györgyi, "The Brain, Morals, and Politics," *Bulletin of the Atomic Scientists*, XX (May 1964), 2.

of its probable consequences. Investing in stocks is not generally considered a particularly moral or immoral activity; it may be prudential (and to a degree moral also) with respect to the future security of the investor's family, and so on, but most of us do not pay too much attention to the remoter consequences of our involvement with the economy. Yet that involvement is obviously voluntary, and if it leads, even indirectly, to a restriction on another man's freedom—to his exploitation or even his death—the responsibility is partly ours.

RESPONSIBILITIES AND RIGHTS. This, once again, is melodramatic language. But there may be some virtue in reversing the usual order of inquiry, to ask not whether I can perform such and such an action with moral impunity, but whether the manifest wrongs suffered by so many people in the world are in any way the consequences of my actions. Although every moral action is performed by a single agent, its consequences are not necessarily restricted to a particular person, and the actions which affect such a person may have been performed by many agents. Morality is a collective as well as an individual matter. If once again we reject the transcendent and supernatural, we are left with the fact that somebody, or some group of persons, is responsible for the present state of the world—for, leaving out of account obviously uncontrollable events like earthquakes and storms, it is evident that man is in charge of his environment, and by now it is certain that there is enough in the way of natural resources to go round, at least for the next generation or two. Whose fault is it, then, that there is poverty and deprivation? It may be retorted that such conditions are nobody's fault, since nobody's actions brought them about. But somebody's inaction failed to prevent them. If a man cannot be free unless he has energy and material at his disposal, and if I have surplus energy and material that I refuse to make available to him, knowing as I do that he needs them and I have no use for them, I have surely acted immorally.

But the argument here is getting ahead of itself. The view that those actions and only those which affect the freedom of others are to be called moral or immoral needs defense, and the most crucial question of all—namely, why ought anyone to act morally at all?—has yet to be approached. My purpose in this chapter has been simply to draw attention to the complementarity of the notions of action and responsibility. If the agent is free in the full sense, then he is responsible for everything which follows from his actions, but morally responsible only for those consequences which are probable and which affect the freedom of others. It is to be noted that if a consequence is probable the agent has already staked his responsibility in performing the action even if that consequence does not in fact ensue. For this reason no separate discussion of *intention* is given here. If we assume that a man's intention in performing an action is to achieve its probable consequences as he understands them, we have an adequate basis for moral judgment, which cannot be evaded by the excuse that what was *really* intended was not the probable consequences at all but some improbable consequence. If the agent is lucky, and gambles successfully for a lesser probability of his own benefit against a greater probability of harm to others, we say simply that he was lucky, not that he acted morally. And if he mistakes the probability of the consequences, either wilfully or in ignorance, we say he was culpable if better information was in fact available to him. I do not deny, of course, that practically there is a difference in the treatment of those who really commit crimes and those who only intend to commit them, but it is a jurisprudential and not a moral difference.

Before closing this discussion it may be worth while to refer to another concept which is sometimes set over against the concept of responsibility, namely that of *rights*. I should say at once that I do not believe that there is any such thing as a *natural* right, a right enjoyed by a man simply because he is a man. A belief in natural rights is possible only in a context of strong transcendent principles (having to do with the divine governance of the world, perhaps, or with the uniqueness and primacy of human existence), and one has only to think of people in danger of being swept away by floods or eaten by wild beasts to see the futility of asserting their unconditional rights to life, liberty, and the pursuit of happiness. Rights come into being in a social setting, and, as has often been pointed out, have their own correlatives, namely duties or obligations. The notion of responsibility reveals another complexity in its relation to rights: the responsibility to do one's duty is different from the responsibility for having done whatever one happens to have done, whether duty or not. The important thing to notice, however, is that it is the individual recognition of moral responsibilities which imposes a moral duty, not simply their existence, and it is the collective acknowledgment of duties which guarantees rights. A declaration of human rights necessarily signifies the acceptance of participation in a human community, the members of which are prepared to assume responsibility for their own actions—that is, to be answerable for the consequences of those actions. If morality were a legal concept, this would be enough for ethics, but from the philosophical point of view it requires more fundamental analysis.

IX
The Idea of a Universal Ethics

THE DEVELOPMENT OF OBLIGATION. Why should we accept moral responsibility at all? We *do* in fact attach imperatives to particular future states of the world, which in the process become values for us, so that (from our own point of view) they ought to be the case. But this does not mean that there are future states of the world to which we *ought* to attach imperatives. The formulation of *that* imperative would read: "It ought to be the case (that I think, or all men think) that it ought to be the case that *x*," and this reiterated "ought" is not so far provided for. The weakness of many contemporary ethical theories is that their analyses are restricted to the second "ought"; they tell us what we mean when we say "*x* ought to be the case" (or "*x* is good," "*x* is right," and so on), but they do not tell us whether that is what we ought to mean, that is, whether we should attach an imperative to a state of the world in which such things are desirable or good or right.

In ordinary language, it is true, the term "ought" is much too strong to be used for the objects of our private desires. I may want something very badly without being inclined to say that I ought to have it. But this I think is a difference of tone and emphasis. Wanting something to be the case and thinking that it ought to be so lie on the same continuum, and not so far from one another at that. It may be argued that wanting is immediate and spontaneous, while the conviction expressed by "ought" is arrived at only after deliberation, and yet it would be easy to think of instances contrary to these generalizations—obligations[1] whose force is almost instinctive, desires which become explicit only after reflection. The difficulty with separating these concepts too radically is that wanting (willing, desiring, and so forth) is the phenomenological basis for value, to which, as was pointed out in Chapter IV, all moral principles must be referred back for their validation, so that to seek some other ground for obligation (such as reason, justice, or social conscience) always leaves open the possibility of flat rejection. If a man does not want justice—if justice simply does not matter to him—no appeal to it will be convincing, and, conversely, those who are con-

[1] A note on the etymology of "ought" and "obligation": "Ought" is from an Old English root meaning "to owe"; "obligation" is from a Latin root meaning "to bind" or "to constrain." Although there is no etymological connection between them, the conceptual connection is of long standing in ordinary usage: "*A* ought to do *x*" is equivalent to "*A* is under an obligation to do *x*." This works nicely as long as *x* is something in or for which *A* has a clear interest or responsibility. But in the impersonal "it ought to be the case that *x*," the corresponding obligation is not so clear.

vinced by such an appeal are those to whom justice already matters and who attach value to states of the world in which justice is realized.

But a man to whom justice does not matter at first may be brought to see that it really does matter. The theory of value, it was said earlier, rectifies the experience of value, just as scientific theory rectifies the experience of perception; and just as the trained scientist perceives the world differently from the way in which the ignorant man perceives it, so the man trained in the theory of value wants a different world from the one the ignorant man wants. Of course, in one sense, and a very fundamental one, the two perceive the same thing (patches of light and shade, shapes, colors, and so on) and want the same thing (for example, sensuous satisfaction or freedom from pain). The difference is that the unanalyzed perception and the unanalyzed desire, which are complex, have, in the case of the man trained in science or values, yielded to rational analysis and been shown to be explicable in terms of universal principles which, when apprehended, are seen to embody more fundamental but equally compelling truths about the way the world is and ought to be. In the light of the theory it is not so much a matter of saying that the object of my private desire ought to be the case, as of making into the object of my private desire what rational considerations tell me ought to be the case whether I want it in the direct sense or not. At the same time I do not have to deny my primitive conations, I have only to reorganize them in a larger context, just as I need not deny that the stick appears bent, but have to place this primitive perception in the context of my knowledge of refraction.

The principle in the light of which my desires have

to be modified, if my behavior is to be moral in the sense of this book, is a principle of the equivalence of human freedoms. It has been shown above that if I want to do anything at all, I must want to be free to do it; in other words, I must attach an imperative to the state of the world in which that freedom is assured. Not, of course, that there is a separate and conscious desire for this state; wanting it is implicit in wanting anything at all, and on reflection may be made explicit, but the primitive phenomenological conation takes no account of abstractions. And if I only want one *particular* thing, all that is implicit is a desire for the conditions necessary for obtaining *it*, so that the argument for freedom does not hold. The assumption is that I want a variety of things, some of them as yet unspecified; in that case, whatever my goal may be, the proposition that I ought to be free becomes a truth for me. What I now need is some way of showing that *other* men ought to be free, and of making this proposition also a truth *for me*. If this can be done then I shall have a rational basis for moral action, a ground for attaching an imperative to the values of justice and equality.

Now to many people the proposition that all men *ought* to be free is as self-evident as the proposition that they themselves *are* free, sometimes even more so, and they tend to be impatient with demonstrations. Their intuition seems to me essentially sound, but their impatience may conceal an awareness of the difficulties involved in any justificatory argument. In this case, as in the case of individual freedom, the best strategy seems to me to be a shift in the burden of proof. Most moral problems arise because somebody chooses to overlook the consequences of his actions as they affect the freedom of others, or because, taking account of the consequences, he nevertheless asserts his right to impose them on others. This generalization has of course to be understood in a sufficiently complex sense if it is to be adequate; the agent may be a group or even a class of persons, the action may be a failure to act, the consequences may affect any of the conditions of freedom laid down in the previous chapter.

We might then try out a preliminary form of the required principle as follows: nobody has a right to disregard the freedom of others. The burden of proof on a person who wishes to deny this is to show how he arrived at the position of privilege in the moral community which entitles him to do so. Only within such a community can the term "right" have any meaning, so that if under attack the attempt is made to shift the burden of proof back again—by demanding evidence for the denial of the right to disregard the freedom of others—it may be answered that however the moral community is constituted (as distinct from the social or legal communities), it is certainly not part of its constitution that a particular individual should have rights which other individuals do not have, and that the alternative universal proposition ("everybody has a right to disregard the freedom of others") would hardly qualify as a principle of community at all, let alone of moral community. To the further objection that the agent in question does not care about the moral community it can only be replied that he is in it whether he likes it or not, and that to claim exclusion from it is really equivalent to claiming a kind of privilege within it. And the force of the principle is equally well expressed if we say instead: there is no privilege, and no argument capable of establishing privilege, in the moral community.

This principle is of an exemplary simple-mindedness,

but in ethics—especially if we remember the conditions for a generally applicable theory laid down in Chapter I—that is no drawback. The principle has something in common with the Golden Rule, the Categorical Imperative, and so on, and this is not surprising. But the Golden Rule is clearly inadequate, since it makes everything depend on the preference of the individual agent (which is all right for art but not for morality), while the Categorical Imperative is much too opaque to be practically applicable. "Act only according to that maxim by which you can at the same time will that it should become a universal law." [2] The obscurities surrounding the concept of universal law and the conditions of its application are enough to reduce the agent to impotence if this is all he has to be guided by. What prevents impotence from being the natural condition of the agent is his own set of conative impulses, but they do not drive him towards metaphysics, they drive him towards concrete and particular states of the world which he sees as values.

THE PRINCIPLE OF INDIFFERENCE. This is of greater importance than may appear at first. Ethics cannot tell men what to do, except in certain special cases, if telling somebody what to do is a way of *initiating* his action. A person who is at a loss for anything to do does not need moral instruction, he needs love or vitamins or psychoanalysis. Most people want to do many things, some of which may have direct or indirect effects on other people, and moral rules are mainly useful in restraining them from doing those things which affect the freedom of others adversely. That is why most moral rules have traditionally been expressed as

[2] Immanuel Kant, *Foundations of the Metaphysics of Morals*, tr. L. W. Beck (Indianapolis: Library of Liberal Arts, 1950), p. 105.

prohibitions: thou shalt not kill, and so on. The world is crowded, and the problem for each of us is to pursue his own ends without thwarting other people in the pursuit of theirs. Sometimes that cannot be helped; if there is only one of something and two people, neither of whom has any antecedent title to it, want it, one of them must be disappointed, and I am not suggesting that the only moral course is to step back and let the other man have it. This might be gentlemanly, but it would not be particularly ethical. It would, however, be unethical to tell him that after all it was not what it seemed, or to hamper by force his access to it, or in some other way to deprive him of the opportunity of fair competition.

Such direct incompatibility of ends is not by any means the most frequent source of moral difficulty, although because of the fact that many interpersonal problems, especially sexual ones, take this form, it is more dramatic and more easily recognizable than most cases of conflict. The deprivation of freedom generally takes place in much more subtle ways. It may be more effective, for the purpose of impairing his freedom, to make a man unhappy than to restrain him physically. It is not so much that unhappiness is painful, but rather that it may destroy motivation and thus inhibit action. To say that inflicting pain is wrong misses the point, as all hedonistic theories of ethics do. Pain is only a symptom; its evolutionary function is presumably to prevent wounded animals from running about and doing themselves further damage, and to induce them to stay still and make recovery possible. Pain following injury inhibits action in order to protect the potentiality for action. Physical or psychological pain gratuitously inflicted on one man by another, however, merely inhibits action without protecting anything, and it is that fact which makes the action morally wrong, not the fact of the pain simply. Similarly lying, fraud, stealing, and so on, are not wrong in themselves but are made so by their probable effect on the freedom of others. There is clearly nothing morally wrong in the enunciation of an untrue proposition, considered simply as such, even if it is done with the intent to deceive; there is similarly nothing wrong in the removal from place to place of a physical object, considered simply as such, even if it does not belong to the person who moves it. Under certain circumstances these actions may become morally wrong—they are quite likely to, in fact. But this is never simply the result of their being the kind of action they are. It is not possible to condemn a class of actions. Moral offenses are committed one at a time, and the intentions and probable consequences which constitute them are not essential characteristics of the actions to which they are attached, but are determined by the conditions in each case.

The principle of the *equivalence of freedoms* on which the foregoing analyses rest may also be expressed as a principle of *indifference between any pair of freedoms* taken at random: there is no argument capable of showing that one man's freedom ought to be exercised at the expense of another man's. The latter formulation is probably preferable, since it reduces the complex case of the maximization of freedom in general to a collection of pairwise cases of the reconciliation of freedoms in particular. In this form, which stresses the symmetry of any situation in which one human freedom confronts another, the principle is anticipated in a well-known passage from Hobbes: "When all is reckoned together," he says, "the difference between man and man is not so considerable as that one man can thereupon claim to himself any benefit to which another may not pretend as well as he."[3] The central point is in the expression "can thereupon claim," which puts the burden of proof in the right place and preserves the status of the principle as a testable hypothesis. It also serves to remind us that if we insist on finite and hypothetical principles, limiting cases may arise to which they do not apply. The principle of indifference maintains that there is no argument capable of showing that one man's freedom ought to be exercised at the expense of another man's. Of course plenty of people have tried to exercise their freedom in just this way, but the history of tyranny and its (so far) inevitable overthrow constitute evidence which, to make only the most modest demands on it, leaves the principle unfalsified. If, however, there were a person capable of coercing others absolutely—an Absolute Tyrant—he could simply ignore the principle and claim all the benefits he liked. In so doing he would put himself outside the moral domain; his behavior would be amoral rather than immoral, and it is worth noticing that this distinction is already current in the case of persons who flaunt the various conventional moralities.

The only possible candidate for the title of Absolute Tyrant in human affairs would be God, and this conclusion is fully compatible with traditional theology. These considerations apply only to one among the conditions for free action, namely the absence of restraint; parallel arguments could be constructed for the availability of information, material resources, motivation, and so forth, leading to an Absolute Deceiver and other analogous beings, each of whom would turn out

[3] Thomas Hobbes, *Leviathan* (Indianapolis: Library of Liberal Arts, 1950), p. 105.

to be God in one of his aspects. Of course God is commonly assumed to be an Absolute Benefactor also, which prevents the misuse of these powers, just as on a human level altruism, sympathy, compassion, and the like can generally be counted on to temper any inclination to extreme ruthlessness or brutality. They cannot, however, always be counted on, and this makes them unsuitable as a basis for morality. It is quite possible for a man to be absolutely selfish or absolutely merciless; it is not possible for him to be absolutely powerful.

THE MORAL COMMUNITY. This analysis is relevant to the vexed question of man's moral relation, if any, to the lower animals. If men are free there can be no doubt that some animals are also free, to a lesser degree (lesser in that their range of possible achievement is, by comparison with man's, much restricted). But if this is true, ought not the principle of indifference to apply to them too? The answer in this case is not quite as simple as in the case of God, but animals may be considered to bear to us a relation analogous to the relation we bear to God: we can afford to ignore their freedom and claim, with respect to them, any benefits we like. In so doing we put ourselves outside *their* moral domain, or, what amounts to the same thing, deny them any rights in ours.

This is not, it must be admitted, a particularly generous attitude to take, although most of us who are not Buddhists or vegetarians do in practice take it. The moral community within which the principle of indifference operates was established by an appeal to the symmetry of human freedoms taken in pairs; the symmetry breaks down if it is a question of God's freedom against a man's, or a man's against an animal's. The Buddhist preaches abstention from injury to all living things because of a belief that life itself is a principle of community, but those who do not share this belief cannot be rebuked by an appeal to symmetry, although a man who wished to exclude another man from the moral community could be so rebuked. (At the borders of that community it may, however, be necessary to exclude or include by a decision rather than by a rational analysis, as is vividly shown in Vercors' novel *You Shall Know Them*, in which an anthropologist is brought to trial and convicted for the murder of a child he has had by a member of a tribe of manlike apes; the conviction confers human status on the tribe and heroic status on the anthropologist, who arranged the whole episode on purpose.)

There are, it is true, stronger and weaker senses of "community." In the stronger sense the members of the community are mutually responsible, either actually or potentially, while in the weaker sense some members may take up a responsibility for others which is not reciprocated. In this weaker sense, men and some animals may be considered to belong to the same community. Animals take no responsibility for the welfare of men, except in special cases (faithful dogs and horses, for example) but many men voluntarily assume responsibility for the welfare of animals. The point about community may be accentuated by the observation that kindness to animals makes sense while kindness to plants would not ordinarily be thought rational. But the consideration of intermediate cases (for example, kindness to insects or to fish) makes one suspect that kindness to animals is more sentimental than rational in the minds of most people. We have a confused sort of empathy for the larger, warmer, and furrier kinds of animal, similar to (and sometimes stronger than) the empathy we feel for other human beings, and this seems morally compelling to people for whom moral compulsion is primarily an emotional matter. The intellect may reinforce the emotions by an appeal to the values inherent in all nature, or something of that sort, but unless we are, like the Buddhists, prepared to take that seriously and extend our altruism to rats and cockroaches, such arguments have a hollow ring.

It should be clear by now that the theory advocated here denies that there are any values inherent in nature—they are all brought into being by conscious subjectivity. It is of the greatest importance, however, to realize that this does *not* mean that human values are the only values. Animals no doubt have their own values, and so do God and the Martians, if they exist. The trouble is that we are trying to devise a practical morality, and we have our hands more than full with human affairs. The consequence of restricting our consideration of values to human ones is, as was pointed out above, that God, the Martians, and the animals are out of the moral sphere altogether. (Considerations of symmetry and consistency would therefore require that nobody who had ever eaten meat or used an insecticide could make a rational protest if a powerful extraterrestrial being of advanced evolutionary status were to decide to make a meal of him, or exterminate his family because their crawling about the newly acquired colony of earth filled the female of the superior species with irrational panic.)

There are, of course, perfectly good arguments against cruelty to animals—it is just that "moral" is the wrong word for them. The child who drowns a cat does something unacceptable, and is punished for it, not on ethical but on social grounds. The punishment is preventive—one day he might turn his attention to other children. Similarly the research worker who becomes indifferent to the suffering of laboratory rats deserves censure, not because the rats suffer (since their suffering may be genuinely necessary for his work, which may in turn be genuinely serviceable for human ends) but because he may eventually become indifferent to human suffering also. If this makes morality sound callous it must be remembered that one of the tasks of this book is to lighten the burden of moral argument (which is at present saddled with responsibility not only for morals but for taste, good breeding, kindness to animals, and so forth), so that it can more effectively perform its fundamental task of preserving human freedom. Morality can only be weakened if its indignation is constantly brought to bear on small boys, butchers, and experimental psychologists.

The limits set to the moral universe by God on the one hand and by animals on the other do not serve to define it quite precisely enough; it is clear that for various practical purposes children, criminals, lunatics, and the senile must also be excluded. Such exclusions must be handled carefully and not made into excuses for oppression; the difference between us and them must be considerable enough to make the asymmetry indubitable, and if there is any doubt, they must be given the benefit of it. The respect in which we treat them differently will in any case usually amount to no more than this—that we shall not feel obliged, when we might for others, to lend them active help in getting what they appear to want. But when all these special cases have been taken account of, the resulting community of men is one in which the principle of indifference can form the basis for a genuinely universal ethics. Such an ethics addresses itself not to all men, but to each man; it calls upon him to recognize that if he is to act rationally he must desire the freedom of others as much as his own, and that if he chooses not to act rationally he reads himself out of the human community, thereby depriving himself of the rights to which membership in that community entitles him. Rationality requires that he be able to give reasons for his actions; the principle of indifference says that he cannot give valid reasons for any action which assigns to his own freedom a privileged status in comparison with another man's. The universality of the system rests on the fact that every man holds his own freedom as a value—an instrumental one to be sure, but nonetheless a value. The applicability of the system to particular cases rests on the fact that freedom is defined in a suitably complex way.

THREE MORAL RULES. It was said above that ethics, as a guide to action, is principally negative, in that it prohibits interference with the freedom of others. But in some cases interference itself can be negative—if, for example, my failure to come to a man's aid when I am able to do so results in a loss of his freedom (which is obvious if he is drowning, less obvious if he is just poor)—and in such cases the guide becomes positive by double negation. There are in fact three kinds of situation in which universal moral principles may be invoked, and three kinds of answer which may be given to an appeal for guidance in action.

(1) If there are, within reach of my causal influence, men whose freedom is restricted in some way (not counting, of course, the exceptions—children, lunatics, and so forth—enumerated above), and if I have at my disposal the resources necessary to remove that restriction, and if I can do so without bringing about a more serious restriction on the freedom of *other* men,

then I ought to do so. The conditions are not simple, but that is no excuse. The dangers involved in this crusading aspect of morality will be treated more fully in the last chapter, but it is clear that the agent must weigh carefully the nature of the deprivation he sets out to correct and the likely side effects of his action for which he may have to assume moral responsibility. If in order to secure for a privileged minority in an underdeveloped country a special form of economic freedom, for example, it became necessary to ravage the whole country and kill many innocent people, the agent of this liberation would be considered to have acted immorally, no matter how praiseworthy his intentions in the absence of the side effects.

(2) If no overriding imperatives of the kind referred to above obtrude themselves—if, that is to say, I have done what I can for the freedom of others—then moral principles have a merely negative force. If my action has any effect on others, that effect ought not to be such as to reduce their freedom. Again it is not a simple matter to decide when (if ever) I *have* done what I can for the freedom of others. Here, as in the case of moral and causal responsibility, the argument needs to be supplemented in such a way as to provide for a pragmatic cutoff beyond which a disregard of other people's instrumental values for the sake of my own terminal ones is justified. (This need for a supplementary calculus will also arise elsewhere, but its provision in any detail will not be attempted, since the principal concern of this book is with the foundations.)

(3) If, under the same proviso, my action does not affect other people, or affects them (within reasonable limits of probability) neutrally, then I can do what I like. Moral principles give me no guidance whatever.

In this situation the theory of value is forced to take up entirely different considerations, which form the topic of the next chapter.

There is of course nothing particularly novel about any of this, except perhaps for the assertion that there are circumstances in which I can do what I like—a hard saying in a society of Puritan origins. (It is to be noticed that the third rule really means what it says: if morality is a wholly interpersonal concept then *if* the conditions are met a private individual can do anything whatever, and so can groups of individuals if they all want the same thing. The two caveats which have to be entered are, first, that it is very hard to be sure the conditions are met and, second, that the fact that an action is not immoral does not necessarily make it admirable or prudent.) The only excuse for reiterating such obvious maxims is that hardly anybody takes them seriously, at least not altogether and in their joint implications. It follows from taking them seriously, for example, that a personally corrupt man who was genuinely solicitous for the welfare of others would be morally preferable to a personally upright man who was indifferent to the welfare of others. The point of that example is not, of course, to defend corruption, but to put the moral emphasis where it belongs, so that the upright but selfish man cannot use his rectitude as an excuse for avoiding moral exertion of other kinds. And it is just one example among many in which the consistent application of the rules would make it clear that many things which have traditionally been considered to matter morally do not, and many things matter morally which have traditionally not been considered to matter at all.

X
The Impossibility of a Universal Aesthetics

CANDIDATES FOR THE STATUS OF UNIVERSAL VALUE. Freedom, as we have seen, is a universal instrumental value; terminal values are to be sought in the ends for which freedom is exercised. Freedom stands for possibility, but this possibility is a possibility of future actualities. The distinction between instrumental and terminal values leads to a separation of moral questions, having to do with freedom, from aesthetic questions, having to do with the ultimate ends served by freedom. Of course in an imperfect world freedom itself may seem a sufficient end, and for a man to devote his own freedom to the task of securing freedom for others has always seemed the most honorable course of action conceivable. But a life spent in such a task would be a purely moral life, not an aesthetic one, and sooner or later somebody must use his freedom for an end beyond itself if so much devotion is to be justified.

It might be argued that possibility itself is the free man's most precious possession, better than any actuality which might emerge from it: to travel hopefully is better than to arrive, and so on. The traveler, however, is hoping for something, even if it is only an ideal and unattainable destination. A future actuality, as long as it remains future, is still a possibility; the aesthetic goal may never be reached, but once conceived it is a particular possibility and no longer possibility in general. As a matter of fact, of course, actualities—works of art, for instance—do emerge, so that this argument is academic. The discipline of aesthetics deals with such actualities and the principles according to which they are and ought to be selected for realization, or the attempt at realization.

A universal ethics is possible, since there is a universal instrumental value, namely freedom. But a universal aesthetics is not possible; it would require a universal terminal value, and there is not a shred of evidence that such a value exists, nor any plausible reason for supposing that it ever could. The conditions of aspiration towards *some* end are laid down, and form the basis for the argument about freedom; but the *nature* of the end is freely posited by the creative imagination, and while investigation into the scope of the imagination might place limits on the range of conceivable ends there is no reason to suppose that, within that range, we would all have to alight at the same point. It does not require creative imagination, of course, to posit certain biological and even intellectual ends common to human beings with inherited constitutions, drives, and so forth; a descriptive study of values actually expressed might lead to the formulation of a kind of universal terminus as the state of the world an ideally rational man would prefer if confronted with the set of all possible alternatives, the state whose realization, therefore, he would devote his freedom to achieving. But this does not take us as far as aesthetics; indeed it hardly takes us further than we have already come. For quite apart from the difficulty of formulating the alternatives (being sure we have them all) it would still be possible to ask: suppose such an ideally preferable state of the world were achieved, what would we want then? One of its characteristics would surely have to be the freedom to seek *further* ends, and this would restore the division between the instrumental and the terminal.

There is, it is true, a strong tradition in the history of philosophy—to which Plato, Aristotle, Spinoza, and Whitehead belong—which argues that there is an end towards which human aspiration moves universally and which identifies this end with God. The variation among conceptions of God already argues against the thesis of universality, but there are more fundamental difficulties. For if God exists he is already actual, and nothing actual can be a terminus of value, except, as we have seen, as men aspire to preserve it, possess it, or in some other way change their own relationship to it—and in this case it is the possession, and so forth, which really forms the terminus. Conversely, insofar as God *is* the universal terminal value, he cannot yet exist. There can be no doubt that the idea of God has been used to justify some of the noblest (as well as some of the basest) of human actions, and has thus served in very many cases as a terminal value, but there is nothing in the situation to warrant a distinction between this value and others as religious rather than aesthetic. If the idea of God has arisen as a consequence of man's striving towards the highest ideals, he may properly be regarded as a work of art; it might therefore be said, without intending a mere parody on Voltaire, that if God existed he would be man's greatest invention. On the other hand, if God already exists he presumably has his own values, among which might be union with his creatures, as theirs might be union with him. But to the extent that this union is conceived as atemporal, it means the end of value as we know it and is properly held at a decent eschatological distance.

I do not intend to deny, of course, either the practical distinction between religion and art or the historical importance of religion to art. Just as the factual content of religious doctrine embodied primitive discoveries about the physical world, while its prescriptive content embodied primitive moral rules, so its ceremonial and liturgical content embodied a primitive concern for art. But the history of art is bound up with religion in a much more intimate way than the history of science or of morals, because the factual and prescriptive aspects of religion are closed—the received truth and the received law cannot be tampered with—while its aesthetic aspect is open to further development. Art, accordingly, flourished under the protection of religion; artistic experiment and innovation, having no cognitive content and thus posing no threat, could be dedicated to the glory of God, while experiment and innovation in science and morals were almost automatically heretical. And art served religion, by satisfying the aesthetic appetites of the people within the institutional framework of the church. The connection between order and value continues to hold here; not only were the moral precepts of the church a reflection of the social order and a guarantee of its stability, but the example set by the church, especially in the lives of the saints (whose importance was far greater in aesthetic than in moral matters), offered to plain men and women a conception of the possibilities for order in their own lives which represented, for many of them, their only opportunity for the practice, as opposed to the passive enjoyment, of art. It is for this reason that the decline of religion has had far more serious consequences for art, in the generalized sense understood in this book, than for morals. Religion, at least in its more formal aspects, is a civilizing influence, and mass culture, largely freed from this influence, has relapsed rapidly into barbarism.

THE NATURE OF ART AND ITS RELATION TO MORALITY. It would nevertheless be a mistake to argue, from these considerations, that religion is necessary to art, any more than it is necessary for science and morals. It is easy to see why so much great art is religious: it is harder to see that it was the art which dignified the religion, and not the other way round, especially since artists have often had a tendency to give God credit for their own achievements. This tendency to underrate human creativity and to assume that, if something noble or beautiful emerges from the average squalor of man's condition, it must be explained by reference to transcendent principles, seems to me unfortunate. Men can and do create order, and the practice of art is the creation of order in its most characteristically human form, an affirmation of freedom and a denial of any dependence.

Art always leads to novelty—never perhaps to anything *entirely* new, since as we have seen every order is only a reordering of what was there all along, and the nature of the artist's material as well as his need to be understood prevent anything like a complete reordering, but never to a mere reproduction or duplication of a previously existing order. Art is the aspect of human activity which most characteristically looks to the future, and to a future which is *not* like the past. (Any art which does not do this betrays the function of art, and in this necessity lies one of the principal differences between art and science, a condition of the success of the latter being that the future should be exactly like the past.) But the work of art need not, although it often does, serve anything beyond itself, or more accurately anything beyond the immediate satisfaction of the artist or spectator. To the extent that the artist has didactic as well as aesthetic intentions he creates something which, while it is no less a work of art, is also something more. Art may have moral implications, but that is not part of its definition as art.

As far as that goes, however, there is nothing to distinguish one manifestation of novelty, which serves no end beyond itself, from another manifestation fulfilling the same conditions. And yet it hardly conforms to ordinary usage to say that *every* creation of order for its own sake is art. Accordingly, aesthetic theory appeals to such concepts as emotional expression and symbolic representation, so as to separate true art from play or aimless doodling as well as from the purely decorative aspects of crafts such as cooking and millinery. But the decorative impulse, like the impulse to play, belongs to precisely the same category as the impulse to create what are ordinarily called works of art, and the products of those impulses should be judged according to the same canons.

The fact that art is usually embodied in works—objects or events occupying space and time—has provided a convenient distinction between it and a good deal of merely aimless activity; *every* object and every action is an event occupying space and time, but a work or a performance has traditionally been regarded as a special *kind* of object or event. Some recent developments, however—pop art, "happenings," and aleatory music—have broken down this distinction by showing that there is nothing sacred about the form that aesthetic activity must take. Even the twiddling of thumbs, if it is anything more than an automatic response to random nervous stimulation, can be brought into the universe of aesthetic discourse.

This is a crucial point. On a higher level the debate must of course continue as to what constitutes good art and what bad, and there is nothing wrong with making the criteria for good art stringent and exclusive—on the contrary. But on the level we are dealing with, the question is: what actions are to be judged according to aesthetic criteria, rather than according to some others? And the answer must be: all genuine *actions* (that is, excluding reflex reactions) which are neither wholly sustaining actions nor judged according to moral criteria; or, in other words: all free actions whatever which are not necessary for survival and do not affect, more or less directly, the freedom of others. As we have seen, some of these actions can be lumped together as ritual or conventional, and in these cases the aesthetic judgment will stand for or against a culture rather than an individual. Such judgments are made less readily now than was once the case, doctrines of cultural relativism having undermined our confidence in our own conventional behavior as a touchstone of value. But if there is to be any aesthetics at all, there may just as well be an aesthetics of culture as one of individual action: the problems they pose are essentially the same. On the other hand, as far as the individual is concerned, conventional actions may be taken as culturally determined, and the problem of his aesthetic life thus simplified.

If freedom serves any end beyond itself, it appears from this analysis that that end must be sought in the realm of the aesthetic. The reason why freedom ultimately matters at all is because it is freedom to seek such an end; and since the argument for morality is that it preserves freedom, the relation between the moral and the aesthetic may be summed up in the following aphorism: *the function of morality is to preserve the possibility of art.* Free men need not create works of art (in the broad sense intended here) but their ability to do so is the badge of their freedom. And this idea is so fundamental that the exercise of this ability may be taken as a badge of their humanity itself.

The trouble with all this, of course, is that it seems to lend support to the kind of aestheticism which says: "I have tried to make my life a work of art," and which indulges in gestures and vanity. When I try to reduce the sphere of the moral to its essentials, and at the same time to enlarge the sphere of the aesthetic, I simply mean that in a materially privileged society aesthetic criteria must be found for the purpose of judging most of what people do most of the time. Such criteria, if properly formulated, would no doubt show that much more of modern culture is ugly than already appears on its surface. But the ugliness with which we have unwittingly surrounded ourselves is not necessarily redeemed by a conscious attempt at the aesthetic life. It is fatally easy to produce bad art by aesthetic concentration, just as it is surprisingly easy to produce good art in the process of doing something else. To put the point in a different way: the end beyond freedom, which freedom serves, is not art; art is the serving of such an end, and the work of art the enduring record of its having been served. The nature of the work very often changes as it progresses, and yet something compels the artist to continue until it is finished or until his interest in that way of achieving his end evaporates.

THE NON-SPECIFICITY OF TERMINAL VALUES. What the end itself *ought* to be is not a matter of dispute, since (as was pointed out above) there can be no universal grounds for the settlement of such a dispute. What it has been in various cases we can learn from the testimony of articulate men in all ages. But already this way of talking is leading us imperceptibly towards the transcendent, by suggesting that in addition to particular ends, identifiable states of the world which are constituted as values, there might be a supreme end or an ultimate value, recognizable as such, which would give a single order and direction to the life of the individual. It would no doubt be gratifying if this were the case, and a good many people have been fortunate enough to find something functionally equivalent to such an end—the Holy Grail, the philosophers' stone—although if they had ever attained it they would no doubt have been quickly disappointed, since the felicity which was to follow the successful consummation of the quest could not possibly, in these cases, be as exciting as the quest itself. Some religious people have cleverly averted the possibility of such disappointments, at least during the course of human life on earth, by putting off the state of felicity until after death; it is usually not clear quite what the conditions of this afterlife will be, but there is general agreement that, at least for the elect, they will be a good deal better than the conditions of the miserable existence to which we have become accustomed on earth.

The prevalence of this idea may provide a clue to the structure of terminal values. Values are future states of the world, but it may be that at first all we know about them is that they are better than the present state of the world; our rejection of the present state sets us off on an exploratory path, along which we are able to recognize states as better or worse than the initial one and to modify our actions accordingly. This process of search is usually guided, of course, by *some* conception of the desired end, as was suggested at the conclusion of Chapter VII; the point is that that conception may be much less specific than was implied there. Blank canvases represent to artists inherently unsatisfactory states of the world. Anybody can change that situation if he has a minimum of equipment, but only the artist knows which changes are satisfactory and which are not. (It has been demonstrated that chimpanzees can paint, some of them rather well, but it is difficult for them to stop painting, and they always spoil their work if a human agent is not present to snatch the canvas away at an appropriate moment.) While even the artist, however, may not always know in detail what order he seeks until he actually sees it, and while the same may be true for ordinary men in pursuit of their own aesthetic ends, it is still the case that we all recognize, with some assurance, states of the world which do embody values and which we therefore wish to preserve. Some empirical generalizations about such states are possible, but only on the crudest level, since what is acceptable depends to a great extent on idiosyncrasies of physiology, taste, education, and so on. It is clear that an individual's values may change, generally in a stepwise fashion on exposure to progressively different experiences, and that in this way tastes may be cultivated and judgment refined. What makes such a change a change for the better is a matter for dispute and lies beyond the scope of this book; it is obviously not possible here to discuss the very complex criteria that separate what is conventionally called "art" from all the other activities to the judgment of which aesthetic canons are appropriate. As far as the conventional meaning of the term goes, this book is not about aesthetics at all.

AN APPARENT CASE OF RETROSPECTIVE EVALUATION. The existence of works of art as valued objects does, however, pose a difficulty for the theory. Art criticism seems to be a pure case of *retrospective* evaluation, since the work is finished and cannot be tampered with, and this appears to contradict the view that value is always future-referential. But here the question really is, not what should be brought into being, but what should be preserved, what should be exhibited, what should be paid large sums for, or reproduced in textbooks, or studied by art students, into the presence of what works should a man take the trouble to bring himself. (Museums dispose works of art in such a way that the value which consists in my having them temporarily incorporated into my world may be realized at will.) All these considerations involve future states, as the theory requires; and it follows that the work of art, regarded as a physical object simply, is of no value whatever. The converse of this proposition, which has been recognized and exploited by artists like Duchamp and Warhol, is that simple physical objects may acquire value if they are regarded as works of art.

In a sense these last remarks might seem like claimants to the status of aesthetic universality, in violation of the denial expressed in the title of this chapter. It should by now be clear, however, that what we are denying is the possibility of a universally *normative* aesthetics, that is, of a universally valid set of prescriptions about the ends to be sought by free action, including the quintessentially free actions of the artist. Aesthetics as the analysis of discourse about art is another matter, and stands as good a chance of achieving universal validity as any philosophical analysis of that type. But by analogy with the familiar distinction in ethics I should prefer to call the latter "meta-aesthetics."

XI

Recapitulation: A General Theory of Value

EGOCENTRICITY AND TEMPORALITY. The preceding chapters have served three purposes. They have dealt, however inadequately, with a number of philosophical problems which must be reckoned with in the construction of an efficacious theory of value—for example, the nature of value as distinct from fact, the freedom of the agent, and so on. They have indicated an essential division of values into instrumental and terminal, and on the basis of this distinction they have limited the possibility of a universal theory to the instrumental (that is, the moral) side. And they have introduced in an unsystematic way the various elements of a possible theoretical model for moral value. The structure of this model must now be made explicit.

First, however, let me make one or two general remarks about the main features of the theory and recapitulate some of the ways in which it is to be distinguished from scientific theory. Its two chief characteristics are, first, that it contains an essential ingredient of temporality and, second, that it is egocentric. It is not on the latter account *humanistic*, however, and this point is of the greatest importance. The theory does not say that man is the necessary center of the universe, but that each man is the contingent center of his own universe; and it does not say that man embodies the highest value, but that each man must decide for himself what the highest value is. The former propositions in these pairs are metaphysical and transcendent, the latter truistic, if not obvious. To claim that each man is the judge of value is only to recognize that, if other men or other beings make judgments of value, it is the individual responsibility of each man to accept or reject those judgments, supposing them to be relevant to his concerns at all; he cannot act on them and expect others to take responsibility for the consequences of his action. To claim that each man embodies a value, while often confused with the claim that each man is the judge of value, is in fact an entirely separate movement of thought, which each man is free to make, which indeed can be argued for on the basis of the theory, but which is not essential to the theory.

What distinguishes the theory of value from scientific theory is the element of temporality, for egocentricity is common to both. The scientific observer is as much isolated in his observations as the agent is in his actions. Observation and action both take place, of course, in a complex human setting; the scientist depends on instruments and on a descriptive language which come to him refined by centuries of development, and the agent similarly makes use of machines and sources of energy, and of a language of request and command, which he shares with the rest of society. But the making of observations and the initiation of action are individual matters, even when the final outcome is such that it can only be achieved collectively. *I* choose to associate myself with a collective enterprise, and *I* have responsibility for my part in it. It may be, of course, that I do not like the enterprise, and go through with it only because of the consequences of not doing so. But it is again my choice to honor the commitment, or to conclude that the consequences of withdrawal would be worse than the consequences of continuing.

This talk of consequences is a reflection of the temporality of value, every voluntary action being taken for the sake of and judged in the light of its probable consequences. While science throws light on the determination of events, the theory of value throws light on the consequences of action. The sequence may be the same, *A* causing *E*, but the value analysis precedes *A*, whereas the scientific analysis follows *E*. If there have been similar cases before, the scientist can predict that *E* will be a probable consequence of *A*; and unless such a prediction is possible, the agent will not know that *E* is a probable consequence and cannot therefore be held responsible for *A* as causing it; so that no *separation* of the range of activity of science and value is possible. The *distinction* between them nevertheless remains: they deal with the same world, but from different temporal perspectives. To put it in another way: the location and the date of a scientific observation do not enter into it essentially—it relates in the same manner to other observations of the same kind whenever and wherever it is made. The location of an observation of value is similarly irrelevant, but its date is integral to it and determines the possibility of its being effectively related to other observations.

Mattering is the phenomenological clue to value, and the behavior of the verb "to matter" is the clue to it in ordinary language. "It doesn't matter" dismisses what is referred to from further consideration, as *merely* factual, or expresses indifference as between alternative states of the world; certain situations "show us what really matters." The etymology here is not helpful, it is true, but the idea is clear: what matters is what is important to us, what we care about, and so forth. Heidegger makes "care" (*Sorge*) the characteristic mark of human "being-in-the-world," something one cannot humanly exist without.[1] We do not choose that things will matter, any more than we choose to exist; they simply *do* matter. We may, under certain circumstances, choose *which* things will matter. We may also come to see that some things matter to which we were formerly indifferent, and that some things we cared for passionately don't matter much after all, but these realizations reflect changes in our situation, rather than properties of things about which we were at first mistaken and then enlightened.

SITUATIONS AND TERMINI. The notion of *situation* is crucial. In earlier chapters the contrast between science and the theory of value was expressed principally in terms of "states of the world," in order to lay stress on the temporal asymmetry involved. Because value enters only from an individual perspective, this was some-

---

[1] Martin Heidegger, *Being and Time*, tr. J. McQuarrie and E. S. Robinson (New York: Harper & Row, 1962), p. 274.

times modified to "states of *my* world." But this latter formulation still preserves a separation between the subject and the world which, while convenient for purposes of analysis, falsifies the phenomenological situation. Situation consists of the individual *in* his world, the world encompassing the individual. When, therefore, we say, in a discussion of questions of value, that the world is or ought to be a certain way, we really refer to the situation of some person or persons. Specifying a situation involves description, but of a more complex kind than that required to specify a state of the world, so that, for example, a change in situation might come about without any overt change in the state of the physical world. The transition from x to y in the expression

$$x + iy$$

introduced in Chapter IV may express a change in the state of the subject instead of or in addition to a change in the state of the world. As far as that goes, the situation of an individual can never reflect adequately the state of the world, since that would require complete knowledge, and it may fail to reflect that state in major respects (for example, a man who has cancer but does not know it) or at all (for example, a patient with catatonic schizophrenia).

The theory of value concerns itself with changes in situation, and hence only with such changes in the state of the physical world as these may entail. The change goes from x to y; it begins because x is different from y and ends when they have been brought into coincidence. The empirical foundations of the theory must therefore be in episodes of this general structure, which have their points of departure in something which "is the matter," as Dewey puts it,[2] and their terminus in some resolution of the initial dissonance. The straightforward pragmatic account is not entirely adequate—there need be nothing conventionally wrong in order to start the process, and it may end without anything's having been put conventionally right. The goal may not, as we have seen, remain constant throughout, but may adapt itself in the course

---

[2] John Dewey, *Theory of Valuation* (Chicago Univ. Press, 1939), p. 33. It may be worth mentioning here the two main respects in which my theory differs from Dewey's. First, for him something's "being the matter" means a *problem;* "desires do not arise," he says, "when things are going completely smoothly." For me, on the contrary, mattering is something which can and does occur in situations having no problematic aspects whatever. Otherwise, value would be a function of the imperfection of the world. We might ask, suppose there were nothing wrong? Suppose every man had his freedom, both positively and negatively, so that nothing stood between him and the object of his desires? If value ceased to be operative under these circumstances we would presumably all commit suicide or at least be intolerably bored. In fact, of course, we would invent new values, new ways of changing some aspect of the world; we would resort to art in its pure form.

Second, and less obviously, Dewey rejects the instrumental-terminal distinction on the grounds that instrumentalities become values in themselves, and that the claim to be pursuing terminal values may be used as an excuse for oppression, since I may consider my terminal values more important than someone else's instrumental ones. It should be clear, however, that the theory presented here would not allow that to happen, since the principle of indifference makes me attach equal importance with my own to the freedom of any other man, and my own freedom is no less a value than any end I can achieve by exercising it. And while it may be that, in the struggle for freedom, freedom itself seems a terminus beyond which nothing matters, still when freedom has been won the question remains of what is to be done with it. It will not do to say that freedom never will be won; that might be contingently true (although I do not believe it is), but the question would still be legitimate, and it could not be answered without reference to some terminus beyond the instrumentality.

of the action, so that a situation which begins unsatisfactorily as

$$x + iy$$

may end satisfactorily as

$$z + iz.$$

(The form of this last expression may be taken as defining the concept of *satisfaction.* I am satisfied when no further change in the situation is called for, and only then—when what is the case and what ought to be the case, with respect to the matter in hand, are one and the same.)

The phenomenological situation may also be described in terms of acceptance and rejection. These are not strictly equivalent to mattering positively and mattering negatively, since one may reject something good for something better, or accept something bad for the want of anything better. But acceptance and rejection provide the dynamics of choice and action. The rejection of a situation ordinarily manifests itself in a movement out of that situation into some other, while its acceptance means the avoidance of any such movement. The movement may or may not be brought about directly by action, since (as was remarked earlier) situations can be counted on to change, sooner or later, if left alone. One possibility for a person who rejects his situation is to *hope* for the supervention of an acceptable one, although the more unusual course is to take action, that is, to *work.* If an acceptable situation does supervene, we may say that the process has reached a *terminus of satisfaction.* If, on the other hand, neither hoping nor working for an acceptable situation succeeds in producing one, the agent can still end the process, in one of two ways. He may cease to hope or work but continue to reject the situation; this may be called a *terminus of despair.* Or he may change his criteria and accept after all the situation he formerly rejected, and this may be called a *terminus of resignation.*

The function of the theory of value is to guide the agent towards termini of satisfaction, and the test of its adequacy lies in its success in doing so, or, if that fails, in its ability to explain what went wrong. But if the test is to be fair the agent must have followed the theory, that is, he must have taken its hypotheses seriously. The test of a scientific theory is its ability to make predictions; but if one of the hypotheses of the theory is that energy is conserved, if the prediction is based on the assumption that the energy involved in the process in question remains constant, and if in spite of this fact the experimenter takes no pains to protect his experiment from extraneous energy, the prediction will probably fail. Similarly, if one of the hypotheses of the theory of value is that *every* man is free, if the guidance offered by the theory requires the agent to take account of the effect of his actions on other people and of their likely response, and if in spite of this fact the agent proceeds as though other people did not exist, he is unlikely to reach the desired terminus. One reason why disagreements in ethics have remained unresolved is that few ethical theories have been thoroughly worked out and still fewer have been put into consistent practice by any number of people over any period of time. Some sets of rules deriving their authority from transcendent principles have had a measure of success, but even there the number of people following the rules faithfully has been small (they have generally been called saints) and the rules have gone by the board when different transcendent principles have come into conflict with one another.

A SCHEMA FOR THE THEORY OF VALUE. Table 2 assembles in one place various elements which have been introduced separately in the foregoing pages, and shows the interconnections between them. It presents more clearly than is possible in a discursive account the moral theory towards which the argument of this book has been directed, but some things about it require clarification. First of all, the four levels differ somewhat from the four levels of Table 1. The distinction made there between the phenomenological and the descriptive is not necessary here, so that they are merged into one, called, for want of a better term, the *experiential*. The theoretical level remains unchanged, that is, the propositions found in it are hypotheses. But the nomological level has been divided into two in the schema. The reason for this is that there are two kinds of rule, the reconciliation of which is one of the major tasks of ethics. There are *ad hoc* rules, here called "inductive strategies," which are generalized from the experience of attempts to satisfy desires, and there are moral rules properly so-called, which are derived from moral principles.

Second, although the hypothetical principles are given explicitly, the rules and other elements are indicated but not given in detail. The function of the schema is to show the structure of ethics, not to present a finished system. Third, the descriptive elements of the individual experience of nature (which enter, it will be remembered, into virtual protocol sentences but not into rules) do not appear in the schema. Learning to cope with them falls under the heading of prudence, not under the heading of morality. The descriptive element is represented, however, by the desires of other

TABLE 2

General Schema for the Theory of Value

Levels	*Descriptive Elements*		*Prescriptive Elements*
Theoretical	Men are free, i.e., their actions can affect the course of events		No man's freedom ought to be preferred to another man's There is no terminal value such that all men should devote their freedom to achieving it
Nomological (deductive)	Definition of free action as: (1) unconstrained (2) materially privileged (3) informed (a) as to the state of the world and (b) as to the laws governing it Laws of psychology and the social sciences, etc.		Rules for the preservation and equitable distribution of individual freedom: (1) injunctions against murder and other, less obvious forms of interference (2) requirement of sharing with respect to natural resources (3a) injunctions against lying and other, less obvious forms of deception (3b) requirement of universal education and access to results of research
Nomological (inductive)	Other people's strategies →	MODIFIED STRATEGIES (some ruled out as immoral or impractical)	← Inductive strategies for the achievement of terminal values
Experimental	Other people's desires	Satisfactions (acceptable termini, modified desires, etc.)	Original desires (raw conations)

people—also, by hypothesis, free agents—which constitute part of the setting for moral action. Fourth, the schema is said to be simply for the theory of value, although it clearly has to do only with moral value. This reflects the conviction, dealt with at length in Chapter X, that only moral values yield to this kind of analysis, aesthetic values (that is, in the language of this book, all terminal values) being incapable of generalization for all men.

The impossibility of a universal aesthetics is in fact embodied in one of the principles of the theory. In addition to the metaphysical hypothesis of freedom, two explicitly normative hypotheses are required. One is the principle of indifference discussed in Chapter VIII, which prevents the abuse of one man's freedom by another for selfish ends, and the other is the principle now under discussion, which prevents the abuse of freedom for transcendent ends. (It must be remembered that a principle is just a hypothesis which is accepted as true.) Both are formulated negatively, which is in keeping with the role of morality in preserving the possibility of free action, and not in any way dictating the nature of that action. The search for positive moral principles, in the sense of directives towards a highest moral good for all men, is vain. For what could possibly be the object of such a search, if transcendent goals (for example, the satisfaction of God in the subjection of his creatures) are ruled out? The highest moral good for me is a situation in which I hinder none of my fellow men from the pursuit of their highest aesthetic goods, in which on the contrary I help them to the best of my power. It cannot include the pursuit of my own aesthetic ends. But this must by symmetry be part of their highest moral good, so that it becomes logically impossible for any man to share in detail the moral obligations of another. He shares them in principle, but the application of principle to individual cases does not lead to *a* highest moral good for *all* men, at least not one that can be distinguished from the sum of the highest moral goods for each.

The deductive consequences of these principles, in conjunction with the definition of freedom given in Chapter VIII, are a series of rules governing the behavior of men towards one another. The *only* moral objectives which one man can entertain with respect to another are in the first place to allow him, and in the second place to assist him, to achieve his own satisfactions in his own way. Here the rules are numbered according to the elements of the definition of free action as they appear in the schema; their practical significance will be discussed in the final chapter.

The deductive movement from the principles through the rules meets an inductive movement from the agent's own desires to a series of *ad hoc* strategies for satisfying them, and it is here that the rectification of desire which is the function of the theory takes place. The agent who has embraced the theory will modify his strategies in the light of the restrictions the theory imposes on him; that is, he will consider whether the strategies are consistent with the rules, *and if they are not he will discard them.* This is the essence of moral behavior. Once again the individual's responsibility is not primarily to follow the rules as positive injunctions; those which are positively formulated, namely (2) and (3b), generally require cooperative action, and their implications, as will be seen below, are mainly political. The function of the rules for the individual agent is to *rule out* certain courses of action, namely those which are inconsistent with the principles. The modified strategies (on which, as the table shows, the whole argument focuses) are the

joint product of the individual's strateg
satisfaction of his own desires, his understandi
a knowledge of their patterns of behavior or
information about their desires) of other peop
probable strategies, and his consideration of the rules. It is quite possible, of course, to modify strategies without considering the rules, taking account only of what other people are likely to do, and taking advantage of their weaknesses. The function of the rules is to engender scruples about that kind of behavior. The unscrupulous man takes a moral risk in ignoring the rules; he is not yet necessarily immoral in fact, although he may very likely become so. And he may be judged immoral in principle, since one of the probable consequences of deliberately ignoring the rules is precisely to become immoral in fact.

THE PROBLEM OF CONFIRMATION. It must be reiterated that this is a hypothetical model, subject to test. If we accept *these* hypotheses as true, and not some others, shall we get the world we want? But what world do we want? The thesis of this book is that in its ultimate sense each of us has to find his own answer to that question, that other people cannot answer it for us any more than we can answer it for them. This being the case we can choose any world we like. But other people will do so too, and we have therefore to come to a point of balance between these free choices. It is essential to respect the autonomy of other people's values and not attempt a Procrustean classification, even in terms of "happiness" or "goodness." (It will be noticed that these terms do not appear in the schema.) What makes another man happy is none of my business, unless he invites me to consider it as such; my observance of moral rules simply clears the way for him to follow happiness if he wants to, to the extent that this can be done without restricting the to follow their own inclinations. cording to the theory that there is e and I must want the same world, ld in which each of us has the best ting the other things he wants. And the claim is that under the assumptions of this theory, namely that no justification can be provided for differential treatment of free agents and that no transcendent objectives are to be imposed, the probability of the values involved is maximized—or, to put it differently, that any systematic discrimination whatever, or any insistence on transcendent principles, will inevitably reduce the probability of the achievement of value for every man. If the verification of this claim presents difficulties, as it certainly does, we are free to follow the strategy for scientific theory and adhere to the principles until they are falsified by evidence. In this regard the theory advocated here has a considerable advantage over most of the available alternatives.

It will be said that the concept of such a theory is Utopian, that the situation is too complex, that the balancing of one freedom against another involves the comparison of incommensurables, and so on. I admit that the analysis needs to be supplemented on the practical level with a detailed consideration of cases, a task for which I am by no means prepared, although I shall try to make a start on it in what follows. But my main intention has been to clarify the rational foundations of morality, and to do this in such a way as to encourage individuals to look to elementary moral principles for the guidance of their own actions. If individual citizens, individual legislators, individual statesmen, were to keep in mind in every action the principle of indifference and apply it honestly for themselves, Utopia would be upon us.

XII

Some Practical Consequences of the Theory

CONVENTIONAL MORALITY. While there is nothing to prevent any individual from applying moral theory directly to his own circumstances, it will frequently happen that the questions of detail raised by the attempt to do this will be too complicated for quick resolution and perhaps too complicated for a decision to be arrived at in time to affect a necessary action. But just as, in the case of natural science, we do not always have to go back to first principles, being able (once we have grasped the structure of scientific theory) to rely on the authority of other people's results without abandoning the ideal of understanding, so in ethics we can follow rules formulated by others without abandoning the ideal of self-determination. The requirement here is that we should understand the principles from which the rules are derived and the conditions under which they are intended to apply. The working out of such rules I take to be the most pressing task of practical ethics. There are already rules, of course—but far too few whose warrant in terms of universally applicable principles is at all clear.

In this final chapter I wish to indicate briefly some of the more obvious practical implications of the theory of value sketched in the foregoing pages. First of all, the usual prohibitions of murder, lying, stealing, and so forth, come out as expected, although not always for the usual reasons. Murder is clearly an ultimate deprivation of freedom, and is therefore categorically immoral. (The problem of killing in self-defense is a perfectly symmetrical one in which the principle of indifference leaves the outcome open; I have no reason to give my freedom precedence over that of the man who attacks me, but on the other hand I have no reason to give his freedom precedence either, and cannot be condemned for taking my own part in the matter.) Lying, however, is not categorically immoral; it is so only to the extent that information required by some agent in deciding on a course of action is withheld or falsified. But it is extremely difficult to know, for any particular lie, that this is not the case, since actions are undertaken in a total context any element of which may contribute to the agent's decision, so that the *prima facie* injunction against lying stands. Similarly with stealing: to remove an object which contributes *nothing* to the material antecedents of free action on the part of its owner cannot be considered immoral, but it is virtually impossible to know that this is the case. The concept of personal property reflects the fact that men have always created a material environment for themselves as a setting not only for free action but also for the sustaining actions which we have seen to be prerequisite to free action, and any wanton disturbance of that environment will have an indirect effect on freedom. The extension of the concept of property to a miserly accumulation of wealth is unjustified because it violates the rule of the equitable distribution of resources. But that is a rule whose enforcement requires collective action, so that individual enterprise in relieving the rich of their surplus possessions cannot be condoned.

Second, however, the theory even in these examples introduces a complexity which simple injunctions cannot possibly reflect. For the freedom of the agent is not determined solely by external considerations, and it may, as has been remarked before, be just as effective —and therefore just as immoral—to restrain a man's actions by destroying his confidence in himself or others, or causing him to be preoccupied with fears or regrets, or simply making him miserable, as by physical coercion or even murder. Any actual realization of individual freedom—in view of the conditions (physical, psychological, social, economic) which must be met, the inhibitions which must be avoided—presents a whole series of opportunities for interference, only the most obvious among which are covered by conventional morality. It is also possible to interfere with the genuine exercise of freedom by encouraging an apparent exercise of it which is bound to fail, for example by making a man want what he cannot have. Freedom in action is always freedom to do a number of particular things, and is thus always relative to those possibilities. I may be free to do *A* or *B* if I choose *A* or *B*, but not to do *C* if I choose *C*, and if somebody who knows this now holds out to me the desirability of

C he acts immorally. Freedom can be diminished just as surely by an enlargement of desire as by a curtailment of opportunity.

CASES JUDGED BY CONSEQUENCES. For the individual, then, the mark of moral responsibility is a sensitivity to the probable consequences of action as they affect the freedom of others. It is not an unthinking adherence to rules of conduct received from society; such conformity only indicates first that the agent has never learned anything for himself and second that he has no *reason* for behaving as he does, apart from the simple and obvious one that this strategy avoids major social embarrassment. But people are always asking for such rules. Are unsanctified sexual relations wrong? Is taking drugs wrong? Is divorce wrong when there are small children? If such actions lead (as they quite possibly will in the first case, and as they almost certainly will in the other two) to physiological or psychological consequences that impair the freedom of some agent—or even in the first case to the creation of a new agent, the conditions of whose freedom cannot be adequately guaranteed—the answer is yes; but a blanket condemnation would clearly be absurd. Again, as in the case of lying, the *prima facie* injunction against the action, which is the rule received from society, need not be discarded, but the agent has to be on his guard lest obedience to the rule should prove a greater immorality than breaking it. It can safely be said that rules of practice always have exceptions, although a general moral rule such as the rule against interference with an agent's freedom has none.

I am aware that this insistence on consequences, the testing of the application of rules of practice (in the light of general rules) for every case, produces acute discomfort in many people. This is sometimes due to a kind of timidity about assuming the responsibility for moral decisions (as distinct from moral actions) which is modest and unobjectionable, although it is no excuse for shirking the responsibility. But such uneasiness sometimes reflects a conviction that no moral life—and perhaps no meaningful one—is possible without guarantees from a transcendent source, that the independent judgment of morality is blasphemous, that the decline of belief in absolute standards is ominous and marks an age devoid of purpose and destiny. This attitude I believe to be pernicious. Purpose and meaning and the destiny of man are where they have always been, namely in the human imagination; it is just that the imagination of the holy men of old, the fathers of the country, and so on, is no longer adequate to the situation, the pace of change having accelerated to the point where every generation needs to redefine these concepts for itself, or come to the realization that they can safely be done without. It turns out that a dogmatic and specific conclusion about purpose, destiny, and so forth on a global scale is more dangerous than no conclusion at all, and it is up to each generation to assert this truth, if necessary, against the crusading zeal of its elders.

IDEOLOGY AND POLITICAL MORALITY. This brings me to political considerations. The theory is politically neutral, as it is ideologically neutral; it speaks of the freedom of men, not of black men or white men, Christians or Buddhists, Chinese or Americans, believers or atheists. And yet the idea of freedom tends to be specialized in the minds of most people as it applies to one of these groups or another, and the term has become a slogan, burdened with all the rhetorical and emotional tasks of propaganda. The "land of the free" in which whole segments of the population demand "Freedom, now!" the war for freedom which deprives a population of its means of livelihood and causes the deaths of many innocent people—these situations are evidence that the concept of freedom is susceptible of radically different interpretations. But it is a complex concept, and these are simple interpretations and therefore partial ones. The most striking illustration of conflict between partial interpretations is provided by the contemporary opposition between two great ideologies, which at the risk of serious oversimplification may be identified with communism and capitalism respectively. The first two conditions of free action, it will be remembered, are the absence of restraint and the availability of material resources. Communism emphasizes the equitable distribution of material resources, but at a price, namely that many individuals should be restrained. Capitalism emphasizes the freedom of enterprise, but at a price, namely that many individuals should be deprived of material resources.

The argument between these theories of social organization has usually proceeded in clichés, and it may be summed up in clichés. Communism, says the capitalist, in its anxiety to liberate the masses (who are often lazy and illiterate) places intolerable economic restrictions on the individual; but a free enterprise economy is essential to the true prosperity of the masses, who ought, therefore, to be content to leave things in the hands of their betters, and discouraged from collective action, if necessary by force. Capitalism, says the communist, in its anxiety to keep the economy competitive (so as to satisfy the greed of the wealthy) allows an intolerable oppression of the masses; but the labor of the masses is essential to the survival of the economy, which ought, therefore, to be considered to belong to them, and expropriated, if necessary by force. I make no apology for the extravagance of this language, which is a fairly accurate rendering of the views of large numbers of people. The opposition extends to the level of definition: Garaudy, a contemporary exponent of Marxism, admits as much when he says, "For the bourgeoisie freedom is the maintenance of free enterprise, for the proletariat freedom is the destruction of this regime." [1]

In practical terms, however, what is more serious is that both systems have resorted to the manipulation of the third condition for free action, namely the availability of information; they have misrepresented the facts about the state of the world, about history, but above all about each other, as may be seen on a cursory inspection of what is taught about communism in American schools, and what is taught about capitalism in Chinese. And the result is that most of the common people of the world, in East and West, and in spite of the protestations of their leaders to the contrary, are in a state of effective bondage as far as their control over their eventual destiny is concerned, bondage unfortunately to men no more intelligent and often less humane than themselves. This situation, which is tragic and unnecessary, can be corrected only by the development of a morally responsible politics—which seems unlikely—or a politically sophisticated morality.

Morality becomes political when its aims can be achieved only by the collective action of a whole society. I can abstain by myself from overt interference with the freedom of other men, but I cannot by myself provide more than a very few other men with the material resources they require to achieve their

[1] Roger Garaudy, *Karl Marx* (Paris: Editions Seghers, 1964), p. 149.

private ends. If I find that I am grossly overprivileged—for example, if I get much too rich—I can do something to put things right by philanthropy, as some of the great financiers of the Western world have done. But to correct the system in which some people get much too rich at the expense of other people requires collective action. It will not do, however, to take such action precipitately—for example by organizing a revolution; there would not be much point in an adjustment which destroyed more than it preserved. (There would not be much point either in preserving from destruction what ought to be destroyed—for example, the unjust features of the system—so that conservatism, the dialectical opposite of revolution, is equally unacceptable. Revolution coerces freedom, conservatism suppresses it; in its radical form each therefore constitutes a morally objectionable basis for political organization.) The same argument applies to the waging of war. It would be too simple to say that war and revolution are always wrong—an intolerable situation might arise which could be corrected in no other way. But if it is categorically wrong for one man to be the moral agent of the death of another, then the parties to a war should be very sure that the benefits to be derived from it, judged according to the universal standard and not according to some local variant of it, are sufficiently great to expiate that wrong. And this is very difficult. It may be that the Second World War was, by this standard, a morally just war. But if so it was perhaps unique.

The chief respects in which political action is necessary are, on the positive side, the equitable distribution of material resources, and the provision of education, that is, the training of individuals to know how the world behaves and thus how to manipulate it successfully. Education, however, has a more complex function than at first appears. If a man knows what he wants, education will teach him how to get it; but if he does not know what he wants (and even sometimes if he does) education may make him aware of values he had not previously entertained, so that he comes to want something (or something else). But what education should studiously avoid is telling him what he *ought* to want; if it does this it is really not education at all but indoctrination. The temptation for those in power to assume that they know what is good for other people is almost overwhelming, but it is disastrous in a free society. The defense of indoctrination always rests in the end on the contention that a man must have certain values because he belongs to a particular society or class—an American cannot be a true American if he is not instructed in the American way of life, a worker cannot be a true worker if the consciousness of the working class is not awakened in him, a man cannot be a true child of God if he is not taught the nature of sin and the necessity of grace. I do not deny that groups of men—Americans, workers, children of God—may entertain genuinely collective values, but I do deny that, at least where the formation of a man's values is concerned, his apparent membership in a group can ever justify an *a priori* judgment about what those values should be. Men must be allowed to create their own values, and thus replenish the world's dwindling stock of them. The values represented by God, history, the nation-state, although they seem now to have the transcendent status which alone would warrant the subordination of the individual to them, were simply human in the first place, conceptions entertained by man as to the possibilities of his own future. We are rapidly using up our inherited futures; technology has in many cases left them far behind already. And we stand in need of new futures.

It is admittedly a great responsibility to be free; Sartre says that "man being condemned to be free carries the weight of the whole world on his shoulders." [2] Human life, it is true, is an awesome business, full of pitfalls; and it ends in death. But, as Spinoza remarks: "a free man thinks of nothing less than of death, and his wisdom is not a meditation upon death but upon life." [3] And within the confines of life he is free to seek his own conception of order, to change his world, inner or outer, to match more closely his highest aspirations for it. It is hard to think of anything less burdensome than that.

If this sounds like anarchy it must be remembered that another collective institution, the law, stands ready to protect individuals from the excessive enthusiasm of their neighbors. Law is the fruit of political action on its negative side. The existence of the law modifies the agent's inductive strategies by introducing boundary conditions which impede the direct gratification of certain desires. There is, it is true, no *moral* obligation on the individual to obey the law, as long as his breaking it is not immoral in any of the direct senses discussed above, but there is a moral obligation (as Socrates showed in the *Crito*) to abide by the verdict of the law, since to escape it would be to claim privilege, in violation of the principle of indifference. The only justification for ignoring the verdict of the law would be evidence that the legal community was clearly not co-terminous with the moral community, evidence, in

---

[2] Jean-Paul Sartre, *Being and Nothingness*, tr. H. Barnes (New York: Philosophical Library, 1956), p. 553.

[3] Benedict de Spinoza, *Ethics*, tr. J. Gutmann (New York: Hafner, 1949), p. 237. This is Part IV, Proposition LXVII.

other words, that the law was giving *systematic* privilege to some segment of the community. All moral activity takes place in a community, and it is necessary to allocate, more or less equitably, the freedom left over when all the restraints imposed by the nature of the community itself have been taken account of. To put the matter in another way, there is just so much causal space available collectively to the members of a community, and the task of the law is to equalize our rights to move about in it. This observation may seem anticlimactic after the euphoria of the previous paragraph—which may itself have seemed cruel to those for whom freedom, in the full sense in which the word has been used in this book, is as yet an unrealized hope.

SCIENCE AND THE AUGMENTATION OF FREEDOM. But here enters the final contribution of science to values. Science, and the technology which accompanies it, manufactures freedom in the form of expanded causal space. It does this in several ways—by prolonging life, by controlling population, by providing economical sources of energy, by devising new techniques of manufacture, by processing and preserving food, by moving things and people from place to place—by continually "doing more with less," to use a phrase of Buckminster Fuller's. If its intellectual function is to help man understand the world, its social function is to help him control it. This is a familiar enough idea, but the question which it implicitly poses is not often enough asked, namely: what is the point of controlling the world? Is it to give a few men a sense of power, or to make a few men rich? To this the reply must be: yes, that among other things; there is nothing wrong with the enjoyment of power or wealth—but surely not that at the expense of the enjoyment of other things by people to whom power and wealth don't matter. It is important to get this point in perspective. The old tags about corruption and the root of all evil are too simple-minded; evil and corruption come not from money and power in themselves, but from the dehumanization produced by the disregard for other individuals which so often accompanies the struggle for these things. But this dehumanization can occur in connection with the pursuit of other, apparently more innocent values, such as stamp collections and flower gardens—or in connection with the pursuit of what have come to be thought of as almost absolute values, such as holiness, or science itself, or even truth, if they serve as terminal values for individuals rather than as instrumental values for mankind, which is often the case.

The moral superiority of shared instrumentalities over private termini is the reiterated theme of this book.[4] In this light the only moral point of having scientific control over the world is to optimize the ability of *every* individual to reach his own private termini—power for those who want power, under the moral restrictions which the facts of competition and the probable consequences of particular actions im-

[4] The moral superiority of the shared instrumentalities is in no way incompatible with the aesthetic superiority of the private termini—but the *theory* of value is principally useful for the rectification of moral, rather than aesthetic, desires. Aesthetic virtues genuinely belong to the class of those that, in Aristotle's language, come about as the result of habit rather than as the result of teaching (Aristotle, *Nicomachean Ethics*, 1103^{b}). It is one of the major misfortunes of the history of ethics that Aristotle himself should have called such virtues "moral," since, as I have tried to show, moral conclusions can be drawn from the intellectual analysis of the situation of free individuals in a human community, which makes morality one of the intellectual virtues. This is not getting an "ought" out of an "is," but getting a general "ought" out of the confrontation of a series of particular ones.

pose, wealth for those who want wealth, privacy for those who want privacy, and so on, under the same restrictions. *And science can do it.* It cannot provide (except for a few scientists) a very useful terminus—that is one of the fallacies of scientism—but it can provide an effective instrumentality, for the control of population and armaments, for the provision of food and shelter for the entire human race. The means are at our disposal for the creation, if not of Utopia, at least of a world vastly more friendly to the individual aspirations of human beings in all parts of it than is now the case.

But this will never come about unless the appropriate values are invoked, and they never will be unless we come to a better agreement about the locus of value in the world and the basis for resolving disputes about it. The crisis described in Chapter II sprang from a failure of transcendent standards of value coupled with a rapid rise of science. Transcendent values, at least those we have encountered so far, do not seem to be able to meet the challenge of science. The attempt has been made here to provide a theory of value having a common root with science in man's effort to understand and control his environment. Such a theory can perhaps serve as a complement to science, by laying down the conditions for the moral coexistence of men in a world served by the achievements of science, so that they may freely pursue human ends of their own choosing. The possible nature of those ends, and the possible satisfactions they can provide, are most adequately foreshadowed by the experience of art in its various forms. But even art cannot be allowed to place limitations upon them.

INDEX

RANDOM HOUSE STUDIES IN PHILOSOPHY

The Moral Point of View: A Rational Basis of Ethics,
ABRIDGED EDITION, by Kurt Baier SPH 1

Philosophy and Education: An Introduction,
by Louis Arnaud Reid SPH 2

An Historical Introduction to Philosophical Thinking,
by Ch. Perelman SPH 3

Philosophical Analysis: An Introduction to Its Language and Techniques,
by Samuel Gorovitz AND Ron G. Williams SPH 4

Scepticism and Historical Knowledge,
by Jack W. Meiland SPH 5

Psychotherapy and Morality: A Study of Two Concepts,
by Joseph Margolis SPH 6

Freedom and Determinism,
edited by Keith Lehrer SPH 7

A STUDY IN PHILOSOPHICAL MOVEMENTS:
The Philosophy of Marxism,
by John Somerville SPH 8

A STUDY IN THE PROBLEMS OF PHILOSOPHY:
The Philosophy of Mind,
by Alan R. White SPH 9

The Concept of Memory,
by Stanley Munsat SPH 10

Science and the Theory of Value,
by Peter Caws SPH 11

Justice,
by Ch. Perelman SPH 12